PENGUIN BOOKS

Meditation Now or Never

Steve Hagen is a Zen priest and long-time teacher of Buddhism. For fifteen years he studied with Zen Master Dainin Katagiri. He lives in Minneapolis and teaches at Dharma Field Meditation and Learning Center in St. Paul. He is also the author of *Buddhism Plain and Simple* and *Buddhism is Not What You Think*, both published by Penguin.

D0309732

Meditation
Now or Never

STEVE HAGEN

PENGUIN BOOKS

PENGUIN BOOKS

Published by the Penguin Group
Penguin Books Ltd, 80 Strand, London wc2r orl, England
Penguin Group (USA), Inc., 375 Hudson Street, New York, New York 10014, USA
Penguin Group (Canada), 90 Eglinton Avenue East, Suite 700, Toronto, Ontario, Canada m4p 2y3
(a division of Pearson Penguin Canada Inc.)
Penguin Ireland, 25 St Stephen's Green, Dublin 2, Ireland
(a division of Penguin Books Ltd)
Penguin Group (Australia), 250 Camberwell Road, Camberwell, Victoria 3124, Australia
(a division of Pearson Australia Group Pty Ltd)
Penguin Books India Pvt Ltd, 11 Community Centre, Panchsheel Park,
New Delhi – 110 017, India
Penguin Group (NZ), 67 Apollo Drive, Rosedale, Auckland 0632, New Zealand
(a division of Pearson New Zealand Ltd)
Penguin Books (South Africa) (Pty) Ltd, Block D, Rosebank Office Park, 181 Jan Smuts Avenue, Parktown
North, Gauteng 2193, South Africa

Penguin Books Ltd, Registered Offices: 80 Strand, London wc2r orl, England

www.penguin.com

First published in the United States by HarperCollins 2007
Published in Penguin Books 2012
001

Set in 12.5/14.75pt Garamond MT Std
Typeset by Palimpsest Book Production Limited, Falkirk, Stirlingshire
Printed in Great Britain by Clays Ltd, St Ives plc

A CIP catalogue record for this book is available from the British Library

978-0-718-19304-1

www.greenpenguin.co.uk

ALWAYS LEARNING   **PEARSON**

I have discovered that all human evil comes from this,
man's being unable to sit still in a room.

– Blaise Pascal

To understand the immeasurable, the mind must be
extraordinarily quiet, still; but if I think I am going
to achieve stillness at some future date, I have destroyed
the possibility of stillness. It is now or never.

– Jiddu Krishnamurti

Contents

PART THREE

For the Long Run

Introduction

As We Live and Breathe

Our lives are lived in thirty-second sound bites. At this moment we are focused on one particular thing; the next moment we are on to something new. We try to stuff in more and more activities, and get more and more accomplished in each twenty-four-hour day. To do this we have created multitasking and the type A personality. We live with the burning sense that we have to get something done.

And yet, what have we accomplished? We can't innovate fast enough to keep up with our own innovative minds. We incessantly produce goods, and incessantly and insatiably consume them, yet we seem never to be satisfied, even as we update our possessions over and over again.

We are like a runner who is leaning too far forward and about to lose balance. Where are we going in such a hurry? Do we really need to be so frantic and driven?

How does this pertain to the practice of meditation? The best way to find out is to do this little experiment:

Find a quiet room free from distraction. In this room, sit still in a stable, upright posture. For a few minutes, just notice the sounds around you, the smells in the air. Notice the feel of the floor underfoot, the feel of your body in a chair or on a cushion or on the ground. Hold a general awareness of your body from the top of your head to the tips of your toes.

Then shift your gaze downward a few feet in front of you and let your eyes relax, keeping them half-open, half-closed.

Notice your breath as you inhale and exhale. Focus on this oscillation. Just follow your breath as it comes in and goes out. That's all – nothing more. Do this for a few minutes.

Afterward, review what you experienced. Did you notice your mind scampering about? Were you distracted? Was it hard to focus your attention on body, mind, and breath? Did you notice an urge to get up and do something?

If so, you're not alone. For most people, the first taste of meditation quickly reveals how we commonly live in a state of constant distraction. Our minds jabber away, flashing images and emotions as if we were fixed on a television set that was permanently switched on. Noises, colors, and personal dramas play out in mental commercials and soap operas all of our own making. We live tuned into ourselves, but tuned out from life.

In meditation we switch the television set off, step away from this busy, hectic mind, and taste the experience of this moment – not as we judge it or comment on it or think about it, but as we live it *now*.

Meditation doesn't only take place when you are seated in

a formal meditation posture. It begins the moment you turn your attention to what is taking place right *here*, right *now*. Thus we can bring awareness to any activity – whether we're at work, playing with our children, eating dinner, washing the dishes, or taking out the garbage.

Meditation begins *now*, right *here*. It can't begin some-place else or at some other time. To paraphrase the great Zen master Dogen, 'If you want to practice awareness, then practice awareness without delay.' If you wish to know a mind that is tranquil and clear, sane and peaceful, you must take it up *now*. If you wish to free yourself from the frantic television mind that runs our lives, begin with the intention to be present *now*.

Nobody can bring awareness to your life but you.

Meditation is not a self-help program – a way to better ourselves so we can get what we want. Nor is it a way to relax before jumping back into busyness. It's not some-thing to do once in awhile, either, whenever you happen to feel like it.

Instead, meditation is a practice that saturates your life and in time can be brought into every activity. It is the transformation of mind from bondage to freedom.

In practicing meditation, we go nowhere other than right here where we now stand, where we now sit, where we now live and breathe. In meditation we return to where we already are – this shifting, changing ever-present *now*.

If you wish to take up meditation, it must be *now* or never.

PART ONE

Getting Started

If we practice meditation as medicine, believing we are sick, it is very difficult for us to realize the true meaning of practice.

– Dainin Katagiri

1. It's About Coming Back

Meditation is very simple. Yet it requires time, energy, determination, and discipline.

Most people think of meditation as a special, relaxed state of mind – one that we maintain for extended periods of time and, with practice, stray from only occasionally. Meditation, however, as we'll first discuss it in this book, is quite another matter. In meditation, we are aware of the frequent wandering of our mind and bring it back, over and over, to the movement of the breath, to the posture of the body, and to itself. We repeatedly return to body, mind, and breath.

This activity, though simple, is not easy. It takes diligence to return again and again to what is taking place, without falling into distraction or agitation or mental dullness.

We are all human beings with human minds. Whether we acknowledge it or not, the human mind is busy and scattered much of the time. It tends to drift off a great deal, often creating difficulty for ourselves and for others in the process.

Our minds all have a profound ability to package Reality into conceptual models – mental representations of Reality. This conceptualizing mind is a great treasure. Our great art, music, literature, and invention, as well as the scientific exploration of the Earth and space beyond, are, in part, creations of this wonderful, incredible capacity of the human mind to package, process, and represent Reality.

Yet we easily get entangled in our conceptualizing minds – in beliefs, ideas, daydreams, and opinions. And we easily lose sight of the distinction between Reality and our ideas about Reality. In the process we miss the true, vibrant life being lived in this very moment, right *here*. As a result of our not recognizing this, we suffer.

Meditation is to leave the clamorous mishmash of our conjured-up world and return to the simple and still clarity of *here* and *now*.

The distracted mind can be likened to a very shallow river. With rocks, mounds of sand, and plants gathering at the bottom, the water passing over the riverbed creates ripples and vibrations. Our mental obstructions don't allow the experience of this moment to flow through, and we suffer turbulence, confusion, and instability.

In contrast, a mind that is calm and aware, that isn't disturbed by passing images, is like a deep river where the water runs smoothly and steadily. The riverbed far below does not disturb the water. In such a mind there is no grasping, and its activity just flows through tranquilly.

The undisciplined mind is easily agitated, nervous, wanting, fearful, preoccupied, distracted, scattered, and confused. In meditation we can begin to see just how busy and distracted our minds really are. We can learn to observe, without judgment, how our minds constantly go this way and that, lunging toward the things we want, and away from the things we loathe and fear. We also begin to see the pain and dissatisfaction that is none other than this leaning mind. And we return to this moment, where sanity, patience, confidence, and openness await – again and again, over and over.

This isn't to say that the leaning of our minds is bad or wrong or dysfunctional, or that we have to root it out and destroy it. There's nothing wrong with our human minds. It's just that we don't usually handle them properly.

In meditation we can see that our thoughts – for all that they obsess us, tease us, distract us, and disturb us – are insubstantial. And with patience, we can learn to hold our thoughts very lightly, like the phantasmagoria that they are.

In meditation we slow ourselves down and observe the activity of the mind. We then see that much of this activity is an incessant monologue of mostly inane chatter. We see that many of the things we obsess over, and that keep us preoccupied, have no consequence whatsoever. We see that much of what we worry about passes away within minutes; indeed, after a few minutes more, we have forgotten what we were so worried about and have moved on to the next temporary obsession.

In meditation we learn to break this pattern. We learn to take care of the mind by observing its dynamics without grabbing at, interfering with, or rejecting anything that comes up.

In meditation we begin *seeing* what we usually ignore – the vibrant Reality in which we all live, all the time – which is to say, right *now*. We begin to loosen our fixation on the thoughts that continuously come up in our minds, like clouds of smoke or bubbles in a glass of champagne. In time we learn not to grasp at the ungraspable.

Meditation is also an expression of faith – not faith in what you believe or what you think, but faith in direct experience itself. Meditation expresses our confidence in our ability to *see* for ourselves the root of human suffering and our trust in our capacity to bring it to an end.

Thus meditation is not something you need to ponder. Meditation is something you do. To truly take up this practice is none other than the actualization of freedom, right *here*, at your permanent address.

2. Why Bother with Meditation

Why bother taking up the practice of meditation when, even in its simplicity, it's so difficult?

As soon as we hear this question, we come up with a list of reasons to justify meditation. We think that we're going to get something from it – that it will lower our blood pressure, reduce our stress, calm us down, or enhance our concentration. And, we tell ourselves, if we meditate long enough, and in just the right way, it might even bring us to enlightenment.

All of this is delusion.

As long as we insist that meditation must have some use or purpose or meaning, or fulfill us in certain ways, we fail to understand it. As my teacher (and many other teachers before him) used to say, meditation is useless.

One of the obstacles we face when we first begin to practice meditation is our desire to know and reap its benefits. 'How can meditation help me?' This approach assumes we are fundamentally sick and in need of spiritual medicine to make us whole. So, when we hear that meditation is useless, that it's not about generating some benefit, we wonder, 'What's the point?'

But if we are to understand meditation (or anything at all), we must drop our preconceived notions, biases, prejudices, and expectations at the door.

Instead, let's look at the mind we bring to this practice. If it's a mind of getting somewhere, a mind that seeks peace, calm, enlightenment, or freedom, then it's not the mind of enlightenment. It's a mind that seeks gain and keeps coming up short, a mind of strain and frustration.

Here is why meditation is useless: meditation is, finally, just to be *here*. Not over there, in some other place called peace or freedom or enlightenment. Not longing for something else. Not trying to be, or to acquire, something new or different. Not seeking benefit.

We need to understand that the wanting mind is the antithesis of the mind of meditation. The mind of meditation is a mind not driven by desires and fears and longings. Indeed, a mind that seeks to rid itself of these painful mental qualities is *already* the dissatisfied and confused mind from which we seek to free ourselves.

When we desire the desirelessness, we remain trapped in desire. When we want the wantlessness, we bind ourselves with yet another chain.

We can't do meditation for any reason other than to be aware. We have to learn to see all of our desires and expectations as the forms of immediate dissatisfaction that they are, and then forget them.

If you're sitting in meditation to get something – whether it's tranquility, lower blood pressure, concentration, psychic powers, meaningfulness, enlightenment, or freedom from the desire for enlightenment – you're not *here*. You're off in a world of distraction, daydreaming, confusion, and preoccupation.

Meditation doesn't mean anything but itself – full

engagement in whatever is going on. It's not about looking for something.

To look for meaning or value is to look for a model, a representation, an explanation, a justification for something other than *this,* what's immediately at hand. In meditation we release whatever reasons and justifications we might have, and take up *this moment* with no thought that *this* can or should be something other than *just this.*

Meditation is not our mental and emotional business as usual. It's about deeply *seeing* what's going on within our own mind.

If we wish to free ourselves from a mind that's tormented by greed, fear, obsession, and distraction, we must first clearly recognize that it's the same tormented mind we are using to blindly pursue meditation. Since we can't throw away this tormented mind, we can instead begin to honestly look at it, with all its expectations, fears, and desires.

In meditation, we do not try to forcefully detach ourselves from the feelings, thoughts, and expectations that arise in the mind. We don't try to force anything into or out of the mind. Rather, we let things arise and fall, come and go, simply be.

In meditation, the things you like come up, then pass, then come up again. The same goes for things you fear or dislike. In meditation we simply see this clearly, without trying to grip or control any of it.

There will be times in meditation when we're relaxed, and times when our minds are agitated. We let both of these states be what they are. We do not seek to attain a relaxed state or to drive out our agitated and distracted mind. That is just more agitation.

When we allow the mind to function and just be *here*, with whatever comes up, without grasping, the mind settles on its own.

If we stay with meditation and continually keep our eyes open, gradually the unhealthy aspects of the mind, including ideas we have about what we're going to get out of meditation, will drop away on their own.

3. Things Mistaken for Meditation

There are many ideas about meditation floating around, most of them inaccurate.

Right now I invite you to put aside any ideas you may have and look at meditation as if you were taking it up for the first time, without any notions or information or expectations whatsoever. Loosen your grip on what you think you know about meditation. Let your mind be open, ready, and innocent, like that of a child. (Actually, such an open, curious, unhindered, and unpresuming mind is already the mind of meditation.)

Meditation is a big word that covers a lot of territory. It's often used to refer to techniques in relaxation, visualization, and trance states. Each of these has a certain value, and each differs from what we'll be looking at in this book. (In the remainder of this book, I'll refer to these techniques by their more specific names – *relaxation*, *visualization*, *trance*, etc. – and save the word *meditation* [and its Japanese translation, Zen] for the practice of awareness, openness, and direct experience of *here* and *now*.)

First, let's try a relaxation technique. Sit down and make yourself comfortable. Take three deep, slow, quiet breaths, and return to normal breathing. But, for the next few minutes, on each in-breath, count 'one' silently to yourself. On each out-breath, again count 'one.' Do this for a while and you can easily notice that, rather quickly, you start to feel calmer. Your blood pressure gets lower, and the stress you feel in your body starts to dissipate.

This is a relaxation technique often taken for meditation. It's very simple, and useful for quickly calming yourself down when you're feeling stressed. Feel free to use it as often as you wish. But it's not meditation.

If your goal is to temporarily calm down, a simple relaxation technique is useful. If, however, you want to experience a mind that is present and collected, this is the mind of meditation. Meditation, in other words, is not a quick fix. It's long-term – that is, it's a lifelong approach to peace of mind, tranquility, and stability.

Visualization is very useful. Many years ago, while being treated for cancer with chemotherapy, and for several years thereafter, I used visualization to improve and maintain my health. Today I sometimes instruct cancer patients and others with illness in the use of visualization techniques.

With visualization, you actively conjure up images in your mind. In meditation, however, there's no deliberate effort to conjure up anything, or to create any mental phenomena. Plenty of them will bubble up anyway, and in meditation, we don't try to hold on to them or drive them out. Contrary to visualization, in meditation we allow our mental images to freely come and go.

*

Unlike relaxation and visualization, which have no significant downsides, the various forms of trance states – sometimes called trance meditations – can be dangerous if you don't know what you're doing. They can even be addictive, like a drug.

In most trance meditations, you turn inward and tune out awareness of your surroundings, your body, and your mind. Your attention becomes filed down to a very narrow, still point, which can feel temporarily blissful.

But every trance is itself temporary. When you come out of it, you're back to all of the problems and confusion that were there when you went into it. There's no transformation.

Gotama, the historical Buddha, mastered various trances in his early spiritual training and came to this same conclusion. He realized that if he entered into a trance while confused, he'd come out of the trance still confused. He realized that if he was going to wake up, trance meditation was not going to help.

We can't deal with our problems by running from them. They not only don't go away, but they follow us and disturb us all the more. We must be *here* to deal with our problems, not somewhere else.

Meditation is not escapism, or tuning anything out. Meditation is tuning in and facing our problems head-on.

Some people think that meditation can help them acquire supernatural powers. Others think meditation will help them build more mundane abilities such as a good memory, or stronger powers of persuasion, or an improved ability to concentrate or to perform their work.

But meditation is not about acquiring anything. In fact, it's about getting rid of the clutter of our mental lives. It's an act of mental housecleaning.

Through our grasping and acquisitiveness, our minds become cluttered with beliefs, thoughts, likes and dislikes, longings and regrets. Yet we don't need to hunt these down, pick them up, and throw them away. If we simply allow the mind to function without deliberately trying to rid it of anything, under the keen eye of awareness it will begin to clean itself.

Bankei was a popular Zen teacher who attracted large audiences. This made a priest from another Buddhist school very jealous, so he came to one of Bankei's lectures to debate with him.

Bankei was in the middle of his lecture when the priest arrived. The priest made such a racket that Bankei stopped his lecture and asked the priest about the noise.

'The founder of our sect,' boasted the visiting priest in response, 'had such miraculous powers that he could hold a brush on one side of the river, while his attendant held a piece of paper on the other side, and the teacher could write his name through the air. Can you do something like that?'

Bankei replied calmly, 'Perhaps your teacher can perform such a trick, but that's not the manner of Zen. My miracle is that when I'm hungry, I eat, and when I'm thirsty, I drink.'

Meditation is not about acquiring supernatural powers. It's about being present and living life completely.

*

When you eat a peach, do you truly taste it? Or do you bite into it, chew it a little, and then swallow it without really tasting it – perhaps while thinking about something else? In meditation, we completely taste, smell, and feel the peach when eating a peach. We totally experience whatever we encounter in *this* moment.

If you're distracted, however – perhaps by thoughts about getting something out of the peach, such as nutrition or energy or enjoyment – your mind will spin off. You won't really taste the peach because you've separated your attention from what's actually happening.

The miracle of meditation is to taste the peach and *know* it directly.

Meditation is about awareness, not about getting something. If you think about what you're getting *from this moment,* you're not *in this moment.*

Another misunderstanding about meditation is that it's a bodily form of philosophical inquiry, a method for breaking through some cosmic mystery to a transcendent reality beyond our everyday world.

Meditation is not about any 'beyond.' Truth and Reality are right *here*, in plain view. They are not vague or far away. Meditation is an acknowledgment and a manifestation of this. In meditation, we *see* that there is no cosmic mystery to break through.

The vivid experiences of sight, sound, smell, taste, touch, and thought are not mysteries. They're clear, vibrant, unmistakable, and ever-present. *Here* is where we put our attention in meditation. We do not give our attention to speculation, belief, ideas, or other mental constructs. This will only leave us with doubt and confusion.

Reality and Truth, which are always intimate, don't require any 'figuring out.' In fact, it's our very desire to figure out Truth that often becomes our greatest hindrance and that most often clouds our vision.

When I was a child, every year we'd have an Easter egg hunt. And almost every time, the last egg found was the one sitting right out in the open on a shelf or a table.

In the same way, it's easy for us to overlook Truth – that is, what's clearly present in each moment – precisely because we're so busily and earnestly looking for it. Thus we're left feeling that our lives are filled with mystery.

If we just attend to actual experience, however, we'll see that life itself is not a mystery. Furthermore, it's our very penchant for digging through all the remote corners of the house for that last Easter egg that leaves us feeling confused and doubtful.

Meanwhile, what we're looking for is in plain sight, for everyone to *see*.

Another misguided notion about meditation is that it's about becoming enlightened.

You can't *become* enlightened. It's not possible.

You can't become enlightened for the same reason that you can't come into contact with Truth: you're already *here*, immersed in it. It's like trying to become human, or searching high and low for air.

When we search for enlightenment, we're like a fish searching for water or a bird seeking the sky.

Enlightenment isn't something you can pursue. And, anyway, you don't need to, because it's already right where you are.

Meditation is not about straining or striving for some special state of mind. It's about letting our habitual striving drop away and simply experiencing what's present before we make anything of it.

Some people have the mistaken impression that meditation is psychologically or spiritually dangerous. Inattention is what is dangerous. Driving your car and not paying attention to the road, to the cars around you, to the stop signs and streetlights, is dangerous.

We go through most of life preoccupied with regrets or nostalgia about the past, or filled with dread or excitement about the future. All of this is distraction from the present, and that's dangerous. When we act out of our attachments, our fears and worries, our unexamined longings and loathings, and our unconscious assumptions, that's dangerous, too.

In meditation we get in touch with what's going on right *here* in our own minds. We begin to recognize how much of what distresses us has no substance to it and is simply generated by our thinking. We begin to see what's causing our problems, and over time, we learn not to be caught by it. This is freedom, not danger.

Some people imagine that enlightenment is dangerous because they fear facing themselves and discovering what may lurk beneath their habitual surface distractions. They're afraid to find out too much about themselves, and worry that what they will find will be devastating or terrifying.

But you don't need to worry about this. Anything you encounter will not come up so fast or so strongly that you won't be able to deal with it. Sure, some of it may be temporarily surprising, or saddening, or frightening, or bewildering. But it won't last if you don't entertain it. If you do play with it, just realize that you're the one who keeps it going. Whatever it is, if you leave it alone, it will dissolve and dissipate. It's not really Real. It's only what you happen to think.

Meditation takes a very gentle approach. Nothing is forced. Just as we have slowly built mental habits over the years, they will drop away at a similar rate. It's a natural process, if we would only not interfere.

We will also discover that much of what comes up that we feared or dreaded is just a phantom, no more real than the boogeyman. When we have the courage to simply look at our own mind, we see that there's nothing to be afraid of at all.

There's also the mistaken notion that meditation is solely for people of high spiritual caliber (whatever that may mean). In fact, meditation is for anyone and everyone. Every conscious human being is capable of it, worthy of it, and fully equipped to do it. If you don't want to meditate, then don't. But don't pretend it's beyond your ability or capacity.

Sometimes people think that meditation is an act of will or discipline or mental striving. Discipline is involved, certainly, but it's radically different from how we usually think of it.

In the practice of meditation, discipline is gentle and even. If we notice that our attention has drifted from awareness of breath, body, and mind, we simply bring it back. That's all.

In meditation we don't try to subdue the mind into silence or prevent it from churning up thoughts through some act of mental force. It would be fruitless, and only serve to intensify the mind's penchant to secrete more thoughts.

It isn't our business to destroy or eliminate thought. We only need to come back to *this moment* – to body, mind, and breath – and not get caught by our thinking. In meditation, we do this over and over, countless times.

The practice of meditation frees us from our insane desire to control ourselves and others. As we continue this practice, doing it over and over again, we discover a mind that is open, magnanimous, and free.

We don't have to fight ourselves to find this mind. As we simply cultivate awareness, all these mental afflictions naturally erode and wash away.

Sometimes people get the idea that meditation is about escaping from our lives, or our painful feelings, or even Reality itself. In fact, meditation is just the opposite. It's about settling down and facing Reality. In meditation we investigate our own mind openly and honestly, without denying anything. We see how we tell ourselves stories about ourselves, about others, and about the world.

It's easy to get caught up in these dramas of who we think we are, who we think others are, and what we think the world is or ought to be. In meditation we begin to see that all of these mental dramas are like puffs of smoke – the buildup of just so much mental pollution that could all blow away with even a single breath of Reality.

Many people come to meditation hoping to experience bliss, euphoria, ecstasy, or some superconscious state of mind. Many spiritual practices and exercises aim at inducing such states. But so can any number of things, both good and not so good – a gorgeous sunrise, rapturous music, sex, street drugs, or even a double espresso.

Meditation is not about creating any particular feeling. Meditation is about awareness, about waking up to Reality.

Some people try to use meditation like a drug, as a way to escape from life or distract themselves from Reality. But anything that draws us away from Reality is deception.

Sometimes people dismiss meditation as a selfish act, something that removes us from life or sets us apart from others.

If you meditate with others, then you are hardly being selfish or isolated in this experience. Indeed, it's best to meditate with others, if possible.

But even if you are the only person in the room, you are anything but isolated. You are sitting on a cushion or chair that someone else made, which is on a floor that other people built. There's the sound of the bird chirping outside. There's the low sunlight dancing on the wall. There's the fresh breeze streaming through the window. There's the whole world right *here*.

In meditation we come to see that we're not separate from others. We come to realize that we're being supported and confirmed by the whole world. This is anything but selfish, anything but isolating.

Furthermore, in meditation we can begin to see through the facade of self, as well as the facade of otherness. We begin to see how selfishness arises, and how easily we get caught up in our petty concerns, desires, hatreds, and fears. Gradually, in meditation all these self-centered thoughts begin to drop away as we *see* the pain that they cause.

Thus meditation frees us from the selfish, greedy mind that troubles us so much. Far from being selfish, meditation is an act of deep appreciation and generosity.

Occasionally, people use meditation to try to experience lofty or highly spiritual thoughts. These thoughts are just more distractions, more forms of delusion.

In meditation, whether our thoughts are lofty or low, mundane or spiritual, we view them in the same way. We allow them, and whatever else comes up, to appear and to pass away. We simply watch our thoughts come and go like bubbles continuously coming up in a glass of champagne. And as we learn to watch our mind, over time, on its own, it begins to settle down and straighten up.

*

Many people, even some longtime meditators, think meditation occurs only in the sitting position, or when we declare to ourselves, 'I'm meditating now.'

This isn't the case. Meditation can take place anytime, anywhere. Being completely undivided, completely in the activity of the present moment – this is practicing meditation. You can do this lying in bed, having dinner alone or with friends, or going in to see your boss.

Lastly, meditation is not a quick cure for anything. It won't magically heal your illness or fix your depression or get rid of your loneliness. It won't provide comfort or solace or nurturing, at least not the kind we typically look for to try to temporarily ease our pain.

Instead, the practice of meditation involves transformation.

I remember, while traveling with my teacher in Japan, entering a little garden. My teacher took a few steps into the garden when he suddenly stopped and pointed to the stepping-stones. 'Stone deep,' he said. 'Step. It feels good.'

It did feel good. The good feeling, of course, was firmness and solidity underfoot. This is just what all of us desire. We want something solid to stand on. Something deep. Something true. Something real.

The practice of meditation is like those deep-set stones. The transformation of a human being who lives this practice is subtle and profound. This transformation does not come quickly, however, and it requires ongoing diligence and effort. It's a continuing process with endless refinements.

Yet through our effort of coming back again and again to *this moment*, where all of us live, we learn *how* to live in this world with sanity, intelligence, and true compassion.

4. Sitting on the Earth

Thus far I've talked about the essence of meditation. Now it's time for you to put this essence into practice by learning formal sitting meditation.

The type of sitting meditation described in this chapter – and discussed in much of this book – is simply following the breath. This is meditation without a lot of moving parts – that is, meditation without any bells and whistles, without analysis, without even counting the breath.

Yet this is not the simplest form of meditation. There is a type of meditation that is even simpler. Known as *shikantaza* in Japanese (or, sometimes, 'just sitting' in English), it is *so* simple that it's best not to begin with it. Instead, we must first learn to calm our minds and to find some stability.

Simplicity is essential in meditation. But simple does not mean easy. It's much easier to have a busy, distracted mind. It's also much easier to take up a lot of complicated, detailed meditation techniques. Unfortunately, most of these techniques eventually get in our way. This is why very few of us wake up.

Let's begin by turning our attention to body, mind, and breath.

Sitting in meditation, we maintain a general awareness

of these three. In this pared-down meditation, the object of our meditation – where we return our attention – is the breath.

We simply follow the breath. If our mind drifts from the breath, we just bring it back to awareness of the breath *without comment*. We keep aware of our posture, the sensations in our body, and the activities of our mind.

It's quite possible to do this while staying aware of the breath – just as it's possible to smell, taste, and feel the texture of food at the same time. In other words, you don't have to drown out everything else to maintain awareness of the breath.

Meditation is something you do. It's not something you just read about or think about. It isn't something you examine from the outside as a spectator. Meditation is something you participate in fully. There is no halfway, no semi-meditation, no 'meditation lite.'

The ideal way to learn meditation is from a living teacher who has years of experience. A good living teacher can answer your questions about meditation and help you deal with problems that may arise in your practice. But the meditation instruction in this book is a reasonable place to start, especially if you can't find a good live teacher.

Some excellent times for meditation are in the early morning, when the day is still quiet, or the late evening, when the day is winding down. But if these times aren't suitable for your daily schedule, find a regular time that fits with your circumstances and devote that time to meditation.

It's best to be well rested so you're not exhausted – but don't skip your regular meditation session just because you're tired. It's best not to meditate on a very full or completely empty stomach – but again, don't skip meditation just because you feel stuffed or hungry.

Always allow yourself enough time to get ready for the meditation. Do not rush, but do not dillydally, either.

Your clothes shouldn't be too constricting. Ideally, they should be loose, neatly arranged, and clean. To the degree possible, don't wear clothes you have just slept or worked in. Do not wear shoes while you meditate.

Find a place that is quiet and free from a lot of distractions. The room should be comfortable – neither hot and stuffy, nor cold and drafty. It also shouldn't be too bright or too dark. It's best if your place of meditation is clean and neatly arranged.

Stability in your meditation posture is very important. Though there are other postures that I will describe in a moment, the most stable postures are on the floor sitting with your legs crossed. So let us begin there.

At the site of your regular sitting, set out a thick mat on the floor and place a cushion above it. Sit on the front part of your cushion, with much of the cushion sticking out behind you. This will allow your knees to come down to the mat, which is imperative. You need stability in your posture, and you will not get that if your knees are floating above the mat. If you can't get both of your knees down to the mat, you can place a low cushion beneath the one you're sitting on, or tuck a low cushion under your floating knee to give it support. If you can't get either of your knees to the mat, you may consider kneeling on the cushion or sitting in a chair. I'll say more on these options shortly.

Sitting on the front part of the cushion also allows you to tilt your hips forward slightly. This corrects your spine allowing you to maintain the natural lumbar curve in your back that you have when you stand or walk. This posture will now give good support to your back and allow you to breathe properly.

In meditation, it's very important to keep your back straight. Imagine being suspended by the back of your head. Your chin will tuck in a little. Don't slouch; you won't be able to breathe deeply. Though slouching may seem more comfortable at first, your back will eventually give out. For the long run (and there's no point in taking up meditation unless it is for the long run), you need to sit with your back straight.

People commonly want to tuck their feet under their knees when they sit in a cross-legged position on the

Figure 1: Half-lotus posture, front view   Figure 2: Half-lotus posture, side view

Figure 3: Full-lotus posture, front view   Figure 4: Full-lotus posture, side view

floor. This is not good; it reduces the stability you need in your meditation posture. It also pulls you into a more slouched position. Remember, unless you're sitting in a chair, it's essential that your knees remain on the mat.

If you choose to sit cross-legged, you have three

Figure 5: Burmese posture, front view   Figure 6: Burmese posture, side view

options: half-lotus posture, full-lotus posture, or Burmese posture.

Here's how to get into the half-lotus posture:

With your knees upon the mat, bring either your left or right heel in close to your cushion, leaving your foot directly upon the mat. Place your other foot on top of its opposite thigh. This gives you a good, stable posture.

An even more stable and balanced posture – although one requiring more flexibility – is the full-lotus posture. To sit in full-lotus posture, begin by placing your first foot on its opposite thigh instead of on the mat. Then place your other foot on top of its opposite thigh.

Figure 7: Kneeling (seiza) posture

If both of these lotus postures are too strenuous for you, you can sit in the Burmese posture. As in the half-lotus posture, bring one foot in close to the cushion, but then place the second foot on the mat in front of the first leg rather than on its opposite thigh. Make sure that both knees are supported, and not floating above the mat.

If the Burmese posture is still too strenuous for you, consider kneeling on the mat (*seiza* posture) with a cushion between your ankles. As in all floor-sitting postures, your knees will be touching the mat. If this is uncomfortable, try putting a second cushion on top of the first, or consider using a kneeling bench (sometimes called a *seiza* bench). As with the cross-legged positions, be sure to maintain the lumbar curve in your spine, and keep your face vertical.

If all of the above postures are too strenuous for you, it's okay to sit in a chair. But not just any chair. Most chairs are sloped toward the back; unfortunately, this will cause some slouching and make it impossible for you to assume a posture that allows you to breathe properly. You need a

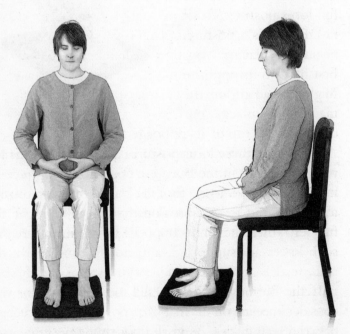

Figure 8: Chair-sitting posture, front view   Figure 9: Chair-sitting posture, side view

chair that doesn't throw you toward the back. Thus you may need to get a special chair just for meditation.[1] (Sometimes people place books on the floor or on the chair seat to make adjustments, but this usually does not correct the slope of the chair seat, which is critical.)

If you choose to meditate in a chair, sit with your feet comfortably close together and flat on the floor. It's important to have your thighs nearly level with the floor – knees slightly lowered. This will maintain the lumbar curve in your spine, giving you good back support and allowing you to breathe properly. Do not lean against the back of the chair; the base of your spine should either not touch the back of the chair or only rest very lightly against it. The upper part of your back should not touch the back of the chair at all.

I recommend placing your cushion, chair, or kneeling bench two to four feet from a blank wall of neutral color. Meditate facing the wall in order to limit visual distractions.

Allow your meditation to begin before you begin formal meditation. That is, even as you approach your place of meditation, settle your mind. Be aware of what you are about to do. Meditation doesn't magically begin the moment you sit down to face a wall, or the moment a bell sounds.

Instead, let your meditation begin even as you think to meditate. If you learn to practice meditation in this way,

---

[1] For information on where you can find an ergonomically correct chair for meditation (pictured opposite), go to www.dharmafield.org/meditationchair.htm.

gradually you will learn to bring awareness to any activity the very moment you turn your mind to it.

Compose your body before entering your place of meditation. Take a moment to stand still and center and balance your body. Place your feet about a fist apart at the heels. Straighten up your spine. Push the back of your head toward the ceiling until your face is vertical – facing neither downward toward the floor nor upward toward the ceiling. Bring your chin in just a little. This will help you stay aware of your whole body.

Gently make a fist with your left hand, but enclose your thumb inside. (With your thumb inside your fist, you can

Figure 10: Standing posture

Figure 11: Detail of hand gesture while standing

be mindful of every part of your hand. Your fist closed around your thumb is also a reminder that it's impossible to hurt others without also hurting yourself.) Now enclose your left fist inside your right hand and bring your hands against your body just below your sternum. Your forearms should be parallel to the floor.

Without tilting your head down, cast your gaze down to the floor at about a forty-five-degree angle, as pictured below.

From this stance, mindfully enter your place of meditation. Be aware of entering the room. *Know* what foot you use to enter the room. Neither rush nor dillydally. Walk to your sitting place mindfully – not slowly, but without haste.

When you arrive at your seat, acknowledge it, silently. (If you like, make the Indian gesture of bringing your palms together in front of you, all fingers vertical with their tips at the level of your nose, and make a slight bow.) Then sit down.

Settle into a steady, immobile, upright posture. Don't strain.

Take one or two deep, quiet breaths. Feel the stability of your posture as you settle into it.

To balance and stabilize your posture even further, place your hands on your knees. Breathe in, then lean deeply to your right as you breathe out, stretching out your left side. Breathe in again as you return to an upright posture. Then breathe out once more as you lean deeply to your left, stretching out your right side. Come back up to the center as you breathe in. Always keep your breath quiet. Repeat these movements two more times, leaning less with each sway.

As you lean from side to side, feel your center of

gravity. Notice it as it passes through your middle. Feel your body settling on the mat as you return to a centered position.

Sit upright, steady and stable, leaning neither forward nor backward, neither left nor right. Take one or two more deep, quiet breaths.

Now, put your hands, open and palms up, in your lap in front of you. Touch the tip of your left index finger to the base of your right index finger just where it joins the palm. Using this as a reference point, lay the fingers of your left hand over the corresponding fingers of your right, palms facing upward.

Gently, bring your thumb tips together until they barely touch. Bring your hands in close to your body, so your thumbs are at or just below your navel. In this position, as you look down, your thumbs should appear above the middle finger of your left hand.

Figure 12: Detail of hand gesture while seated

With this gesture you form an oval with your hands. This hand gesture (sometimes called the 'universal *mudra*') is particularly sensitive to both your posture and your mind, so it will alert you when you have lost your concentration or your vertical posture. If you become agitated or caught up in thought, your thumb tips will tend to press together, forming a peak. If you become drowsy, your thumbs will likely fall and the oval shape will begin to collapse. If you notice either of these in meditation, simply return your hands to the shape of the oval.

You will also not be able to keep this delicate oval shape in your hands if your posture is off. A mental scan of your hands will inform you of your posture in general.

Take a deep, quiet breath.

Now, without tilting your head forward, cast your gaze downward at a forty-five-degree angle. Your line of vision should strike the floor at about the same distance in front of you as your eyes are above the floor. If you are sitting facing a wall, your line of vision may intersect the wall.

Let your gaze fall in a general area. Do not fixate on any specific point. You should be able to see clearly while meditating. Because your gaze is downward, your eyes will appear to be half-closed, but keep them comfortably open. Just relax your eyelids, and they will naturally settle into a half-open position.

Your eyes should always remain open during meditation. This is often difficult for people new to meditation to understand. But, remember, meditation is not about tuning out the world, but about awareness.

Close your mouth in a normal fashion. With your lips and teeth both shut, place your tongue against the roof of your mouth, with the tip of your tongue just behind your upper front teeth. (Your tongue will likely go here quite naturally, but in meditation, we keep it there. This keeps your mouth from filling with saliva, and it actually helps to settle your mind and enhance your concentration.) Breathe gently and quietly through your nose. (If you are congested, it's okay to breathe through your mouth.)

Place your mind on your breath. Be aware of breathing in as you breathe in. Be aware of breathing out as you breathe out. Don't force your breath in any way. As your mind and body settle, your breath will naturally deepen. Breathe with your diaphragm, so as you breathe in, your abdomen will swell out, and as you breathe out, your abdomen will move in.

Breathe naturally. Don't think about it. The length of each breath may vary slightly; that's fine. Don't try to control your breath; just follow it. Allow your breath to settle deeply into your body.

As you meditate, even for a short while, you will notice your mind wandering about. It picks up on sights, sounds, and smells in the environment and runs off in daydreams, thoughts, and analysis. It jabbers to itself. Feelings and thoughts arise, one after the other. This is normal and natural.

When you notice that you have slipped off into thought and not been mindful of your breath, just come back to the breath. Do not judge or comment on the fact that your mind checked out. Just come back. There's no need to criticize your scattered mind. It's enough to just notice that you've drifted from the breath, and then to come back.

Most of us live out our lives without realizing just how scattered our minds actually are. As we go about our daily business, much of the time we're not *here*. This becomes starkly apparent when we sit down and try to follow our breath.

So don't be alarmed by the fact that your mind often wanders about when you sit in meditation. Everyone's does – at least at first. In fact, until they learn to be present, this is how almost everyone's mind operates virtually all the time.

Now that you've begun to notice how scattered your mind is, however, you can learn to come back. *You can't come back if you don't notice that you've run off.* So don't let your noticing interfere with your meditation.

Your mind wanders away, and you bring it back. It wanders away again, and you bring it back. In meditation, we do this repeatedly. Cultivating and maintaining this awareness *is* the practice of meditation.

With practice, over time, your trips away become shorter, less frequent, and not as absorbing. Gradually you learn to reside where you actually live – *here* and *now*.

In the beginning, if you have a lot of trouble maintaining concentration – that is, staying with the breath – try counting the breaths.

There are different ways to count the breath for various effects, but the simplest way is to silently count 'one' on the in-breath, 'two' on the out-breath, 'three' on the next in-breath, and 'four' on the next out-breath. Count up to ten in this way, then start over again with one. If you lose track of your counting, simply begin again at one. Do this until your mind settles down and you can once again follow your breath without counting.

It's best to let go of counting the breath as soon as you feel you can do so – because, over time, even counting the breath can become a distraction from *here* and *now*.

*

Suzuki Roshi, like any Zen teacher, encouraged his students not to change position while sitting. In the book, *To Shine One Corner of the World*, he said, 'Don't move.' But then he added, 'When I say don't move, it doesn't mean you can't move.'

This is excellent instruction. It allows us to function in a manner that is firm and yet not rigid.

The rule is 'don't move.' But by itself, this is extreme. Still, this isn't license to move. Don't move just for the sake of mere comfort, but if you're very uncomfortable, quickly and quietly adjust your posture. If you have to sneeze, cover it in the crook of your arm. When moving is unavoidable, don't try to avoid it. Otherwise, remain still.

Like two countervailing forces in dynamic balance, these counter instructions help to keep us from drifting off into the extremes of being either too rigid, or too lax. Neither should be forgotten nor indulged.

When the meditation period has ended, place your hands on your knees. As you exhale, lean slightly and slowly to the right. On your next inhalation, return slowly to the upright position. As you next exhale, lean slightly to the left; return to the center on the in-breath. Keep your movements smooth and slow. Repeat these sways two more times, increasing the range of each one, until on your final sways you stretch out each side of your body. Keep your movements definite and graceful. Be mindful.

When you get up from sitting, move slowly and quietly, calmly and deliberately.

*

One of the most common questions I hear is, 'How long should I sit?' I will discuss this further in a later chapter, but for now it's enough to say that you should sit for at least ten minutes, but probably no more than forty minutes. What is far more important, however, is that you sit with regularity. Once a day, or three times a week, are good places to start. I would not recommend that you sit any less frequently than that. You can always increase the length or frequency of your sittings later on. But you want to arrange a schedule that you can actually stick to. This is what is most important.

Everything about this form of meditation has been cultivated and refined over many centuries to accomplish these two characteristics of mind: calmness and awareness. This upright posture of sitting firmly on the Earth is to remain alert without agitation, and to experience a mind that is both stable and aware.

5. Walking on the Earth

We sometimes call formal sitting meditation simply 'sitting,' but this shorthand can be misleading. It's certainly possible to assume a seated meditation posture – and appear to most outside observers to be meditating – yet to be completely caught up in a whirl of thoughts and mental images.

It's also quite possible to meditate – that is, to be fully present in *this moment* – while walking, lying down, engaging in conversation, watching the moonrise, taking out the garbage, or doing anything else. In fact, as we shall see, with experience meditation is less and less something we *do*, and more and more something we *are*.

This chapter is about meditating while walking – not walking to go from one place to another, but walking as the experience of *here* and *now*.

How often do we allow ourselves to appreciate what a precious experience it is just to walk on the Earth? If you were suddenly deprived of that ability, what would you give to get it back? When we walk in meditation, we give ourselves the opportunity to fully realize and enjoy this simple, common, profound, and yet commonly ignored activity.

In meditation, we fully realize what a marvelous experience walking is and feel grateful for it all: the shift of our weight, the stretching of our legs, the feel and creak of the floor or the soft, earthy smell of moist ground underfoot.

Sitting still isn't terribly hard, but it can sometimes result in stiffness or pain, especially if you sit for prolonged periods. For this reason, I recommend meditating while seated for no more than forty minutes at a time. If you'd like to meditate longer, walking meditation allows you to get up and walk about without breaking focus.

At Dharma Field, the meditation center where I teach, our morning and evening meditation sessions usually run eighty minutes: thirty-five minutes of sitting meditation, ten minutes of walking meditation, and another thirty-five minutes of sitting meditation. Although most people would find eighty minutes of continuous sitting quite painful, most have no trouble with this 35/10/35 arrangement. (When we have *sesshins* – two to seven full days of meditation – we reduce the sitting periods to thirty minutes each.)

In our group walking meditation, because our cushions are facing the walls, we walk the perimeter of the open floor just inside the line of cushions, very slowly, taking one small half step per breath. If you're meditating on your own, you may walk in a circle around the room.

Some teachers and traditions encourage meditators to walk at a normal pace, or even faster than normal. My own training, however, has been to walk at a very slow pace, and my experience suggests that this best supports a quiet and steady awareness, especially in a group.

Walking meditation is quite simple. As with sitting meditation, you need to be shoeless. Begin by taking the standing posture described and pictured on pages 36 and 37.

Follow your breath in and out while in this standing posture for half a minute or so. Then, on your next in-breath, when your lungs are almost full, slightly lift your right foot from the floor – first the heel, then the ball, then lift off with your foot nearly level. Bring your foot forward a half step, so that the arch of your right foot is slightly ahead of the toes of your left foot.

Touch the floor first with the ball of your right foot and begin breathing out gently through your nose. Slowly shift your weight to your right foot as you exhale, touching your heel to the floor last.

At this point, you will naturally begin inhaling once again. As you continue to slowly shift your weight onto your right foot, midway through the shift, your left foot will now begin to come off the floor at the heel. (You are still bearing weight on the ball of your left foot to maintain your balance.)

When you are about to exhale again, your weight will be balanced over your right foot. You can then lift your left foot entirely off the floor, lifting off from the ball, yet keeping the foot nearly level. Take a half step forward, so that the arch of your left foot is slightly ahead of the toes of your right foot. Make contact with the floor with the ball of your left foot and begin exhaling.

Continue this process breath by breath, step by step. There should be continuous forward movement and a continuous shifting of your weight from foot to foot as you walk. This gently stretches and exercises the tendons and ligaments of your legs, while enabling you to maintain a quiet and focused state of mind.

Walking meditation also helps you with your concentration since you're constantly shifting your weight and periodically balancing on one foot as you move the other foot forward. You need to be constantly focused to coordinate the continuous shifting of weight and to time the balance point (when you lift your foot from the floor) with the turning of your breath (when you again make contact with the floor). Thus it's a good exercise for developing your sense of balance, as well.

If you are doing walking meditation with other people, try to maintain an even distance (at least two or three feet, if possible) between you and the people in front and back of you. Continue to take one step per breath, but regulate your speed and distance by the size of your steps.

If you're in a line or circle with others, it's also important to be mindful that you're not lagging and thus causing a backup behind you. Lastly, be aware of the line or circle of people as a whole so as to even out the space between people.

Is it possible to carry out walking meditation in a public place? Yes, though I don't recommend the very slow one-half-step-per-breath method, which might cause others to wonder about your sanity, simply because it is so unfamiliar.

Instead, try the following, which resembles an ordinary stroll through the park.

Let your arms hang loosely at your sides. Walk forward at any comfortable but unhurried pace. Whatever your pace, however, take the same number of steps on each in-breath as you do on each out-breath. This is crucial for maintaining both rhythm and concentration. For instance, you might take eight steps per breath – four on each inhalation and four on each exhalation.

Look straight ahead and down at a slight angle so your gaze falls in an area roughly ten to twenty feet ahead of you.

This will probably not feel natural to you at first, but it will enable your attention to stay with your walking at this faster pace. Gradually, over time, this way of walking will begin to feel more natural.

Count your paces silently to yourself – 'one, two, three, four,' on the in-breath; 'one, two, three, four,' on the out-breath – but only until you establish a rhythm. As soon as possible, leave off counting and just walk mindfully, maintaining an equal number of steps for each inhalation and exhalation.

After you've built up some experience with walking meditation, try this: during a normal walk through a park, or along a trail, or on the beach, instead of letting your mind ramble through a multitude of random thoughts, see if you can return to *here* and *now*, moment after moment, time after time, just as in sitting meditation. You will discover that it is quite possible to practice walking meditation, making all the correct turns, without ever having to comment to yourself on anything at all.

I'm not suggesting that you walk mindlessly, as you might on a casual stroll or a routine walk – such as on your daily walk to the coffee shop a couple of blocks away. You've done that routinely for so many years that now you do it without ever attending to where you are or what is going on.

This is not what I mean by not commenting to yourself on anything. On the routine walk described above, you are *not* fully present. In walking meditation, you *are* fully present and aware of where you are and what is going on. You are just not commenting to yourself on any of it – or anything else, for that matter. You are only wordlessly remembering to walk mindfully on the Earth.

6. What's Your Problem?

Let's consider some of the problems that people often experience when they first take up the practice of meditation. (Note that most of these are problems we all routinely face not only in meditation, but also in our day-to-day lives.)

Difficulty getting into a sitting posture

Some people are naturally more flexible than others. It may take you awhile to become flexible enough to settle into a stable posture. That's fine. It's not unusual for some folks to take a couple of years before they can get their knees down on the mat.

So don't get discouraged. With daily sitting, gradually you'll get the flexibility you need. (Unless, of course, you are limited by an injury or other physical ailment, in which case you may consider sitting in a chair.)

Stretching before meditation helps. Any form of stretching will do, though you may find basic yoga very helpful.

Pain

Pain is a common experience in meditation. But pain can also provide some rich nourishment for us.

Pain can teach you how to practice. Indeed, it can teach you how to live.

Of course, serious or extreme pain is not good, and should be avoided. But having no pain at all is not ideal, either, because sitting in meditation with no pain provides no background resistance to work with.

This isn't to say that we should go out of our way to create pain and difficulty for ourselves. But in the experience of pain, we have an opportunity to learn a valuable lesson. Lanza del Vasto noted that pleasure teaches us that it is not what we should seek because it continuously runs from us whenever we chase after it. Similarly, pain teaches us that it's not what we should avoid because it has much to teach us about life.

If you do have pain in sitting meditation, by all means take reasonable steps to minimize it. There's nothing wrong in this. Bear in mind, however, that it's only when we desire not to have pain that pain becomes a problem for us.

When you do experience mild or moderate pain or discomfort, remind yourself to observe it and not to run from it. You may notice that there are actually three things going on in your mind. First, there's the raw experience of the pain itself, and then there's your resistance to that pain. There's also the mind that wants to run away from the pain.

If you don't attempt to eradicate the pain, you'll learn something vital: that your ability to deal with pain increases if you don't put energy into ending or avoiding it. You'll see that it's not the pain that's causing you difficulty. It's your resistance and your fighting with it that causes so much trouble. It's only when we try to get outside the pain that we define the pain as 'bad' and make futile attempts to escape it.

With careful and honest examination, we will eventually see that what we're actually resisting is our *idea* of pain, not pain itself. As we resist pain, pain only seizes us with greater force. But if we're fully present with the sensation of pain – and if we notice our resistance – we can learn to let the desire to escape weaken and wither away.

Legs falling asleep

There's a common misconception that numbness in our legs in seated meditation means that we're cutting off the circulation and thus damaging the body. Excessive numbness is not good, of course, and steps should be taken to correct that should it occur (I'll get to that shortly). But worrying about slight or intermittent numbness is not necessary. In thirty years of teaching meditation, I've never seen or heard of a single case of gangrene or phlebitis caused by sitting meditation.

A slight amount of numbness is not unusual. If, however, the numbness is excessive, or if you have trouble standing up or walking (even for a short while) after meditation, consider changing your sitting position. Go from full-lotus to half-lotus posture, or from half-lotus to Burmese or kneeling posture. Or try putting a second cushion under your regular cushion. This sometimes helps, but avoid sitting atop a pile of cushions. It's important to maintain stability in your posture, so you don't want to elevate yourself too high off the floor. You may also try sitting in a chair.

Sometimes people experience numbness in their legs because their cushion is overstuffed or understuffed. Numbness in the legs can also be caused by the way you're seated on your cushion where, without changing your posture, a slight shift of the cushion may be in order.

A small amount of numbness may be unavoidable. While it's not necessary (or good) to tough things out, watch for the mind that merely wants to escape *any* discomfort.

Weird sensations

Occasionally as you meditate, you may feel as if your body is getting larger or smaller. Or, you may temporarily lose track of your shoulders, hands, or legs.

These sensations are all very common, and very temporary, and they are, of course, illusions. Just continue to follow your breath. Your normal bodily sensations will return by and by – certainly by the time you get up from your cushion or chair.

Sometimes during meditation you may feel that part or all of your body is off balance. Usually this is simply a variation of the strange sensations described above. Once in a while, however, you may, in fact, be a bit off balance. Without moving, mentally do a quick body scan. Just become aware of your body. Check your hands

– not by lowering your head and looking, but just rotate your wrists slightly, or bring your thumbs together. Move your shoulders imperceptibly, just enough to regain awareness of your body. As you regain a sense of your body, adjust your posture as necessary.

Hallucinations are also not unusual. These should not be taken as a sign of spiritual insight, or of your 'third eye' opening. It's not a sign of mental instability or illness, either. It's simply your mind attempting to entertain itself. It signifies nothing. So if you see faces or bunny rabbits appearing before you on the wall, just blink your eyes or slightly adjust your body to come back to normal sensations. Then turn your attention back to body, mind, and breath. You're just sitting there. This other stuff is only going on in your mind. It's just mental static. Forget the magic show, and simply maintain a general awareness of your body, from the top of your head to the tips of your toes.

In meditation, especially for beginners, such weird sensations will sometimes come and go. There's no need for alarm, but don't indulge them, either.

Drowsiness

If you become drowsy in meditation, be aware of that sensation. Don't try to jolt yourself awake, but don't let yourself drift off to sleep, either. Watch how this state of lethargy arises and how your mind begins to sink into it.

Make an effort to remain alert. If you become drowsy, check your posture. If it's not upright and stable, this may be contributing to your drowsiness. Adjust your posture as necessary, and be sure to keep your eyes open.

One simple technique to help you deal with drowsiness is to temporarily reverse your breathing and the movements of your abdomen. Usually, as we breathe in, our abdomen swells out, and as we breathe out, our abdomen moves in. Try doing the opposite for a few minutes: on the in-breath, pull in your abdomen instead of letting it balloon outward, and on the out-breath, let the abdomen swell out. After a few such breaths, return to the normal flow and movement of breathing.

If drowsiness is a common problem for you, examine your lifestyle. Perhaps you're not getting enough sleep, or not taking enough breaks during the day. Maybe you're getting *too much* sleep. Experiment and adjust as necessary.

Eating a large meal and/or drinking alcohol just before meditation can cause drowsiness. Let at least an hour or more pass between eating or drinking and meditating.

Boredom

Boredom can be interesting. If you find boredom interesting, you cease to be bored.

Looking at boredom is much like viewing our problems. If we look at boredom with curiosity, boredom no longer seizes us. Curiosity, openness, and investigation cure boredom.

What's happening when we're bored? We've ejected ourselves out of *this* vibrant experience and into our own heads, so to speak. If we're bored, we're not present but drifting away in thought. You can't be mindful and bored at the same time.

But what if, mindful or not, we *do* get bored in meditation?

First, we should just notice the boredom. As we look at it, we will see that it is not a physical state, but a mental fabrication – a desire to be somewhere other than right *here*. Then we try to run from boredom by looking for something to busy ourselves, or distract ourselves, or entertain ourselves. We're bored by boredom – by our own failure to engage fully with *here* and *now*.

Over time, if we patiently observe boredom, however, we will eventually discover boredom's flip side – wonder and creativity. Indeed, lightning often strikes from boredom's grey cloud.

We can learn to practice patience in the midst of boredom and wait for it to pass, as we would an overcast sky. We can learn to let these different states of mind come and go by taking quiet interest in what is taking place *now*. And while at first we may think not much is going on, with careful observation we may begin to realize a whole world beyond our petty lives unfolding in every moment.

There's no boredom *here*. And no room for the tight confines of our usual self-preoccupation. There's only vibrant life and freedom.

Distracting thoughts

All kinds of thoughts will bubble up in meditation. Some will be mundane, some surprising, some delightful, some disturbing. Let them all arise and fall.

Whatever thoughts come up, don't resist them. Resistance will only intensify thinking. Just let the thoughts crop up as they will, and they will die down or drift away on their own.

Learn just to *watch* your thoughts without comment. Put your bare attention on the thoughts without adding anything.

The unruly mind doesn't like to be watched. But if we *just watch* our mind without commenting, even to ourselves, our mind will begin to straighten up and settle down on its own.

Strong emotions

Emotions can bubble up in meditation just as freely and unpredictably as thoughts – and they can (and should) be dealt with in exactly the same way since they are virtually one and the same. Let them come up, but don't cling to them. Then *simply watch* as they dissolve – as they eventually will if you do nothing more than observe them.

Suppressing strong emotions doesn't work. We become like a pot of boiling water with a lid tightly secured on top. It's only a matter of time before we explode.

On the other hand, continually expressing those emotions doesn't work very well, either. After venting, we may feel relief temporarily, but we haven't truly dealt with them.

In meditation, if a strong emotion – intense anger, for instance – arises, just look at it. Notice if you are trying to suppress it. Notice if you are trying to pump it up further. Then simply be aware of what results.

If we watch our mind in this way, in time potentially destructive emotions will begin to subside. We'll less frequently reach our boiling point – and, even if we sometimes do, it won't last as long as it once did. It will be like the natural dying down of a hurricane once it moves inland from the shore.

Resistance

Regularity is the cure for resistance to practice. When it's time for your regular sitting meditation, just sit in meditation. If you feel resistance rising, know that it's not unusual. Go ahead and feel that resistance. Look at it. And then continue your regular meditation schedule, resistance or no resistance. Don't let it take you away, or it will only strengthen.

If you can get past resistance to meditation, nothing else in life will be an obstacle. If the worst situation comes to you, you can deal with it. If the best situation lands upon you, you can continue to walk steadily. Over time, resistance will become but an echo in the mind.

Be honest and attentive with whatever resistance does come up in your mind. Face it down, and it will cease to be a problem. With regular practice, resistance will evaporate like dew in the early-morning sun.

Discouragement

Discouragement is unfulfilled expectations. It results from getting stuck in how we think things ought to be. To the extent that we are discouraged, we are not actually present. We're caught up in our ideas.

If you're discouraged, just return to right *here*. *This place* – right *here* – is where we can have no expectations. There is satisfaction with whatever comes up. When you totally engage your life, you'll not experience discouragement.

We all have problems. We don't like our job. We have difficulty with our kids. We have to fill out our tax return. The list is endless. Even when our life is humming along beautifully, we still have three big problems to face: we get sick, we grow old, and we die.

According to a parable of the Buddha, we each have eighty-three problems. No matter what you do, you will always have eighty-three problems. If you work very hard to remove one of these problems, another one will take its place. In other words, as long as we're alive, we'll always have problems.

But the Buddha also noted a very common eighty-fourth

problem: we don't want to have any problems. This is the one we can deal with.

We usually view our problems as things to get rid of, so we can at last arrive at a place and time where we are problem-free. This is how our kicking and screaming mind tries to escape difficulty and pain.

But this is precisely the wrong approach for anyone who would live a happy, sane, and peaceful life.

We can't escape problems. But we can *see* them in a radically different light – at which point they cease to be problems.

Problems are like weeds growing in our garden. But weeds, when properly dealt with, can become fertilizer to enrich our garden. Problems can be nourishment rather than irritations and annoyances. Problems can be opportunities for us to grow and to learn.

If we're stuck in our problems, it's because we're trying to run from them – and from our life. If we feel frustration or desperation, it's because we're trying to push our problems away. Sooner or later, however, we'll hit a wall, and we'll have no choice but to face our problems.

Our only way out is to take in our problems and be nourished by them.

In meditation, we look unflinchingly at our difficulties, the looming mental entities that we don't want to face. We see them clearly and undeniably in the floodlight of awareness.

And then, as we watch, they begin to weaken and dissipate – and we can *see* that the very things we've so desperately avoided are nothing more than phantoms, mirages, and unpleasant dreams.

In other words, what we habitually react to is not Reality, but our *take* on Reality. It's within our own hearts and minds where our problems are created. And it's within our own hearts and minds that we can find freedom.

Ultimately, in *seeing* clearly the workings of our minds and the ephemeral nature of our ostensible problems, we'll find a profound freedom that will never depart.

7. The Three Legs of Meditation Practice

There are three essential elements to meditation practice: regularity, meditating with others, and non-judgment. All three are necessary if your practice is to mature and flower.

These three work together in countless ways. For instance, regularity is made easier with the help and support of others. The ability to refrain from judgment is supported by the power of regularity. And the realization that we're never separate from others, whether in meditation or in life, grows naturally out of the ground of regularity and non-judgment.

These three aspects of meditation work together as a whole, in the same way that a three-legged stool needs all three legs to provide support and stability.

Let's look at each of these aspects of meditation in detail.

Regularity

Meditation practice is for life. It's not something we take up for a quick fix or temporary relief. The practice of refining the mind has no end. Because we continuously encounter new (and often unexpected) circumstances, our ongoing task is to return to *this moment* with awareness. There's no transcendent end-state we'll eventually arrive at where we'll no longer have to be present and to practice awareness. *Here* is where we'll find sanity, peace, and the ability to deal with whatever comes up.

Regularity is our ability to be present. With regularity, our practice develops strength and stability, as awareness penetrates all facets of our life. Thus, the work of meditation, and of living our life, is endless. In each new moment we can live in either awareness or ignorance.

This is why regularity in meditation is so critical. Without it, we tend to fall into worn patterns and habits that spring from an undisciplined and egocentric mind – patterns and habits that create pain and difficulty.

There will be times during your meditation schedule that you just won't feel like doing it. This is normal. It's all too easy to justify why today would be a good day to take off. In this and innumerable other ways, we kick and scream and try to avoid meditation.

In such moments, it's all the more essential that we practice with regularity. When our mind resists following our meditation schedules that's precisely the time to stick to it.

We need to forget how we feel and what we think about meditation at the moment, and just take up the practice.

If we're honest with ourselves, we'll immediately know the difference between a legitimate reason for missing meditation and a flimsy excuse. For example, maybe a friend needs a ride to the airport during your regular meditation time. By all means help your friend, but then resume your regular schedule. On the other hand, if you go looking for friends to drive to the airport, you're looking for ways to avoid meditating. Similarly, if you're too sick to get out of bed, then stay in bed. Your health is important, and if you're contagious, it's wise to stay home. If you're sick, you're sick. Be aware of your situation.

Be honest with yourself. You might be making up excuses to avoid meditating. The point is to notice what you're doing.

Reality doesn't care how we feel at the moment. And, when it comes to meditation, neither should you. If it's time to meditate, it's beside the point whether you're bored, or tired, or shaky, or upset. In fact, it's in our very resistance that we create suffering.

Over time, if we practice regularly and honestly, our kicking and screaming mind will subside. We'll learn to walk evenly through life and not to be perturbed by the events we encounter. We'll discover that we are well equipped to deal with whatever unwanted situations come our way. We can engage fully in our life with equanimity. We can experience each moment for what it is, as it happens, without emotional residue.

Eventually, with the discipline of a regular meditation practice, we discover an underlying joy that resonates with us even as we ride the ups and downs of life. No matter where we are, no matter what we encounter, there's nothing we can't face. We find true courage and strength – not an artificially manufactured courage where we foolishly put up a front in dangerous or difficult situations. We learn to return to this moment and to honestly, unflinchingly investigate it. We pay attention to our life and learn to *see* all things with an unbiased eye. To practice meditation is to live with patience, strength, vitality, and genuine fearlessness.

People new to meditation often ask me how long they should sit in meditation in a given period. This matter of how long is not the critical point. The critical point is to put regular times for meditation into your schedule – once a day, three times a week, twice a day – and stick with them. It's also essential to have a definite beginning and ending time. If you have determined that you will meditate for twenty minutes every morning, then commit to a regular starting time and an ending time, and then do it.

Our meditation practice reflects the attitude we take in life. If our practice is unstable or based on our whims and impulses, our life will follow in the same way and become ever more difficult – even unbearable. In short, if we're serious about taking up meditation, procrastination and vacillation have to go.

Regularity teaches us to take one step at a time and to take care of our life in each moment. Regularity also teaches us to be reliable and trustworthy, to keep our word. Regularity in our meditation practice thus develops habits of mind that will make our lives worth living.

Meditating with others

My meditation teacher used to point out that the Chinese character for sitting meditation depicts two people sitting on the Earth. This illustrates how we should understand meditation practice: as inseparability from others. As we meditate, we're *here* – in the universe, on the Earth – with all beings.

You cannot meditate in your own egoistic world. If you're caught up in yourself, you're not meditating.

One reason why it's important to meditate with others is because it reminds us of how we actually live in this world. It shows us how our life is interdependent with the lives of all beings. In meditation, we step outside of ourselves and into the vast, open space of selflessness.

Meditating with others also sustains the practice of regularity by providing solid (if silent) support and encouragement. Practicing with others helps us to continue despite our feelings of resistance.

Practicing with others stabilizes us as well. Others can mirror us and show us when we get lost or confused or caught up in our vain imaginings. And we, in turn, reflect and stabilize others. As our practice deepens, we come to see just how important this is.

Lastly, meditating with others – and especially with the guidance of a meditation teacher – can help to keep us sane.

This doesn't mean that you should never meditate without other people present. Many people meditate in their own homes on a regular basis, as well as with a group when they can – perhaps two or three times each week or month.

Although meditation functions best as a communal practice, *you* are the one who has to make an effort; nobody else can do it for you. Only you can live your life. Yet meditation flourishes with the recognition that we can't really practice alone.

Non-judgment

In meditation, we refrain from passing judgment. Judgment, as opposed to discernment, takes us out of the present moment and into our heads, where we assign weights and values to everything and then fixate on our evaluations. To the extent we're fixated, our minds have become brittle, rigid, dogmatic, and inflexible. In short, a judgmental mind is antithetical to meditation.

In meditation, we stop picking and choosing. Instead, we only observe without comment. We don't label, evaluate, or judge. Or, if we do, we let go of that label, evaluation, or judgment as soon as we notice it, and return to *here* and *now*.

The key to refraining from judgment is to be curious, but not to latch onto anything. Just observe as the phenomena of the mind come and go. Question everything, but judge nothing. Just remain engaged and open, and *see this* as it is.

As we learn to refrain from passing judgment, we can begin to go easier on others, and on ourselves as well. Over time, we also stop judging how we're doing in meditation. This judgment only pulls us out of the moment. There will be moments when we experience the mind as calm and tranquil. But if we then slip into judgment ('Wow! This is a great meditation!'), we only break our concentration and leave *here* and *now* behind. Judging our meditation can also lead to discouragement when, the next time we meditate, we discover that our mind is now busy and scattered.

This is where non-judgment and regularity work together. If we have a 'bad' meditation session, in which our mind will not settle, we may become discouraged and want to quit. But our practice of regularity, coupled with non-judgment, will keep us going in spite of our discouragement (which is, after all, just another delusion).

In refraining from judgment, we find a flexible, open, and tolerant mind. The awareness we develop by practicing in this way gradually expands to reach out all around us. Ultimately, it includes everything. Thus we learn to live with a magnanimous heart.

Practiced together, these three essential elements are the heart of a deep, steady, lifelong meditation practice. Meditation is, above all, to settle down and to live life intensely, yet calmly, with awareness – with energy, yet with ease.

8. Bringing Meditation to Life

To sit silently on a cushion in a quiet space, bringing full attention to body, mind, and breath may seem one thing, while being stuck in bumper-to-bumper traffic, trying to get your sick mother to the doctor for an appointment for which you are five minutes late already, may seem quite another.

How do we practice awareness when we're off the cushion and smack in the middle of the commotion and stresses of daily life?

If we practice formal meditation for thirty minutes a day and leave our sanity, patience, and clarity on the cushion, we don't really understand what meditation is.

In order to realize the subtle depths of meditation, we must learn that we have an opportunity in every moment for sanity, patience, and ease.

Practiced sincerely and regularly, meditation permeates your life and enters into every activity. This transformation will not occur, however, if you don't have the intention to awaken in *this* moment. And then in *this* moment, once again. And *this* one.

Waking up can take place anywhere. *Now*, as you're on your way to the meditation center in your car. *Now*, as you're walking up the steps to the door. *Now*, as you take off your shoes and place them mindfully on the shoe rack. *Now*, as you read this sentence. It's simply a matter of making the effort to be awake. *Now*, not later on. *Now*.

Meditation is doing one thing and doing it completely. If you're driving, then driving can be meditation. If you're taking off your shoes, then taking off your shoes can be meditation. Meditation is doing *this* activity in complete awareness.

At the heart of meditation is the intention to be awake. This intention has no room for thoughts or desires, hopes or fears, fantasies or plans.

If we are to awaken to our delusion, we can want only one thing – Reality as it is, before goals, ideas, or desires sprout.

Meditation is a commitment to Reality. It is the pure desire to engage in life as it is, not as we hope or wish it to be.

In each moment, we must make a choice: do we want Reality or something else? This is the only true choice that is ever available to us. And it's total. A matter of life and death.

9. Bringing Your Life to Meditation

Many years ago, on a beautiful fall evening, I received a great lesson in life – one that helped me to realize the right attitude toward meditation.

I arrived at the meditation hall, settled in, and sat facing the wall along with a few others. The golden light of the setting sun flooded the room with a soft glow. There was no wind, and all was still, quiet, and calm. Then, out of the calm came the sound of running. Distant at first, the footfalls became ever louder as they approached the meditation hall.

It all unfolded in sound: the crash of the outer door, the ripping of Velcro, the shoes dropping noisily to the floor, the rattling of coat hangers, the hurried steps into the meditation hall. Then, amid huffing and puffing, the clear sound of the meditation bell rang out, and everything settled back into stillness with the fading of the bell.

I was suddenly struck by how we bring ourselves to meditation. In that moment I realized that we need to be in meditation even before we come to meditation. It's not just the contradictory notion of 'hurry up and meditate' that is wrong. It's the notion that meditation doesn't begin until the official starting bell rings – and the parallel notion that whatever happens after the bell rings, including frantic thoughts of 'Thank goodness I made it in time!' constitutes meditation.

Sometimes we approach meditation as if it were either spiritual muscle building or a slightly painful virtue, like eating canned spinach. At other times we may view meditation as a necessary chore, or as punishment, or even as penance. We feel we have to do it for our spiritual health – whatever that might mean. We think we need it, as if we're sick and in need of vitamins or medicine. 'I *need* to sit,' I often hear people say. 'I'm so stressed out and ungrounded.'

But meditation is never a means to an end.

At the meditation center where I teach, we regularly have eighty-five-day practice periods, as well as more rigorous one-hundred-day training periods during which people commit to a regular meditation schedule. This can help them in establishing a regular meditation practice. All too often, however, people view the schedule primarily as an ongoing obligation to fulfill, as if it were a part-time job. They think meditation is about putting in time on the cushion.

As a result, participants in the practice periods sometimes ask me for time off, or try to bargain with me, as if I were their boss or supervisor: 'I have to go out of town for a conference next weekend; is it okay if I miss Sunday meditation so long as I meditate at my hotel?' Or, 'I wasn't here yesterday because I had to see my dentist. But I can meditate extra next week; will that be okay?'

Well, sure, it's okay. But it's a fundamental misunderstanding of what meditation is. 'Can I skip being *here* and *now* tomorrow morning if I'm *here* and *now* a little extra on Thursday night?' That's what people are really asking – and, as you can see, it's a contradiction in terms. This misunderstanding is virtually universal among beginning meditators. If left unexamined and unresolved, it will ultimately contribute more to discouragement with meditation than any other factor.

A regular meditation practice is an outward manifestation of the way your mind functions. Is it stable, focused, present, and aware, regardless of where you are, what you're doing, and whether or not it's an 'official' meditation period? This is a far more pertinent question than 'Can I have some time off from *here* and *now*?'

We don't meditate according to a punch clock. If you're truly meditating, you're not thinking, 'Now I'm meditating.' If you notice your mind has slipped away, just bring it back.

But, of course, if you notice it's slipped away, in that instant you've already come back. This is meditation.

10. The Ins and Outs of Breath

In meditation, we commonly focus our attention on our breath.[2] There are many reasons for this – some simple, some quite profound.

First of all, wherever you go, your breath is always with you. It's constantly available.

It's also portable. You can't get away from it, or forget it, or leave it behind. This makes meditation possible wherever you are.

It also helps to keep meditation simple. If you forget about the breath, you can always find it quickly and easily once again.

Breath is free. It's already yours. You don't have to acquire it, or search for it, or order it from a catalog.

Breath is always immediately *here*, and always alive.

Breath doesn't entangle us in complexities of thought or emotion. No one declares themselves pro-breath or anti-breath. No culture looks down on breath or declares it immoral. Unlike focusing on, say, a cross or a Buddha statue, no one feels in awe of it or infatuated with it or repulsed by it.

Breath doesn't distract us, or incite us to spin out in any direction. It doesn't thrust us into any particular state of

---

[2] After some years of experience, many people meditate without any particular focus at all, even on their breath. I'll discuss this in detail in Chapter 35.

mind, such as alarm or delight. Instead, it helps us to find stability.

Using breath as the object of meditation also helps us avoid getting caught up in greed, longing, anger, repulsion, or delusion, the sources of virtually all human difficulty and suffering. When our mind leans toward certain things and away from others, it's unstable, perturbed, and unsettled. Following the breath helps us to not chase after – or to run from – these mental projections. Instead, it helps us to settle into *this moment*.

Where we find peace, contentment, and stability is never 'out there' or in the future, but right *here*, right *now*. And in returning to the breath, we invariably return to *here* and *now*.

Breath doesn't have to be conjured up or mentally constructed. The fact that breath is not like this makes it easily recoverable when our attention strays.

Another aspect of breath is that it unfolds in time, continuously shifting and changing with each moment. It has no particular form, whereas if we focus on a visual or mental object, it readily appears solid, graspable, and unchanging. Breath is nothing but change, flux, and impermanence – and thus more directly reveals the very nature of Reality itself.

Breath is like a swinging door. In any given moment it shows us something new. Yet, despite its ever-changing quality, it is ever-present. It continues through all the turmoil of our thoughts, actions, and emotions. Breath changes, yet it never goes away.

There's yet another vital quality that makes breath truly

unique – and that makes it the ideal focus for meditation. Breath is both objective and subjective at once. Nothing else in our world is quite like this.

Breath is ours to easily control, if we desire – yet we can forget all about it and it will continue to function. We can find it in an instant and observe it like an object, yet it's an intimate part of us at the same time. (In comparison, our heartbeat can be difficult to locate and follow, and it is much harder to control voluntarily.)

Uniquely, breath rests on the apparent boundary between the inner, personal, subjective world – the world 'in here' – and the objective world 'out there.'

Why is this so important to meditation? Because we can learn to place our attention on this supposed boundary line. As we do this, over and over, gradually that line begins to blur. We begin to see that there isn't such a clear distinction between inside and outside, between 'me' and 'not me.'

Over time, breath leads us into the deeper aspects of meditation. As we shall see, breath is thus a passageway to sanity, intimacy, wisdom, and compassion.

PART TWO

From Day to Day

We cannot put off living until we are ready. The
most salient characteristic of life is its urgency,
'here and now' without any possible postponement.
Life is fired at us pointblank.

– José Ortega y Gasset

And don't forget – forever is always now.

– Josh Baran

11. Constancy

In Chapter 7 we looked at the three legs of meditation practice: regularity, meditating with others, and non-judgment. These are essential to practicing meditation over the long run.

And so, in this chapter, and the two that follow, we'll look at these three aspects of meditation in more detail, in order to see and feel their vital importance.

Constancy is the single most important factor in maintaining a meditation practice. If you find constancy in your practice, it's like throwing a switch that allows everything else to follow. Without it, there will be no understanding, no enlightenment.

Meditating only now and then, when the urge arises or when you've had a stressful day and feel you need it, is like trying to boil water by turning on the stove for thirty seconds at a time, whenever you're in the mood. Unless the flame is constant, the water will never boil. Yet even a low flame, if maintained long enough, will do the job.

Constancy means meditating no matter how we feel or what we think at the moment. We just go ahead and practice, no matter what.

Without this attitude, we're just treating meditation the

way we treat most everything else. Mentally and emotionally, it's just business as usual.

In any moment, of course, we may lose our way or get distracted. But as soon as we remember, we come right back, take up *this moment*, and carry on – without giving another thought to having just slipped off. This is constancy.

People new to meditation often misunderstand constancy. They think it's about not faltering, not losing your way or focus. But constancy is *precisely* about faltering, over and over, and coming back, over and over.

With this understanding, we let ourselves be human, allow ourselves to err and to learn, and avoid getting discouraged about our meditation practice.

So it's not that we never veer from the path, but that we waste no time in returning to it. No time for discussion. No time for excuses. Back to *here* and *now*.

To establish constancy in your practice, it's essential that you set up some kind of regular meditation schedule. Just as creating a budget helps us with our finances, a regular schedule will help you with meditation.

This schedule might be as simple as half an hour every morning just before breakfast. Or maybe it's twenty minutes at midday or twenty minutes before bed on workdays, thirty minutes each morning on weekends.

It's best to meditate at precisely the same time every day. Building a regular schedule around meditation creates a solid and grounded daily routine that brings stability to your life and allows you to maintain a steady, ongoing practice. Making and *keeping* this regular appointment from day to day is to put your entire life in order.

The most important thing to remember is to set a schedule that you can actually follow, not one you dream of following. Often when people first take up meditation, they are excited about it and overdo it, perhaps setting up a schedule that is too ambitious. This might work for awhile, even a few years, but if it's too much, it will only undo itself, and perhaps much of your life as well.

Even if it's modest at first, it is far better to set up a schedule you can stick to without much difficulty. After you can maintain this schedule for a few months without missing any scheduled times, you can gradually increase the amount of time you devote to formal meditation practice. The key is to never waver from the schedule you set unless you are ill, or faced with an emergency, or some other unusual situation. As my teacher used to say, life is daily routine *and* unexpected occurrences. To live in constancy is to take care of both.

The ideal schedule pushes you slightly, creates just a little internal resistance. This is good grist for the mill. Without some resistance, your practice will likely atrophy and die away; with too much, you may get discouraged and give up.

As long as you stay with your schedule, the meditation practice will mature. Over time, you may increase the amount of time you spend in formal meditation. And as you continue to push gently against your resistance, your practice will gradually become more subtle and profound.

*

Sometimes people think they are too busy to meditate. But how can you be too busy to be present?

Meditation isn't a vacation from life. Meditation is simply being present – even in the midst of tasks and obligations, urgencies and emergencies. Having a busy schedule is not a valid reason to avoid meditation. Indeed, in taking up meditation wholeheartedly, you may discover it's not necessary to be quite so busy.

When we practice constancy and meditate without internally fussing or complaining, our whole life begins to change. Whereas before we might have resisted getting out of bed in the morning, now we just get up. This is much easier than lying in bed dreading the thought of having to get up and face the day.

With constancy, we learn to take care of *this moment* whether or not it is something we want. If *right now* it is time to get out of bed, then we just get up. If *right now* it is time to go in for cancer treatments, we just go in. We're not tossed around by circumstances. We just get on with life.

Over time, you will come to *see* that this is the easiest, freest, sanest way to live.

12. Sitting with Others

Our ordinary understanding is that each of us meditates in a universe filled with lots of other people and things.

But what kind of meditation is this? *I* entered the meditation hall. *I'm* sitting in meditation now. *I* am concentrating. *I* am distracted. *I, I, I, I, I.*

This notion that we meditate as separate individuals simply is not true. It's not possible to meditate as a separate person. We are *always* interacting with others – or, more accurately, with the Whole universe – whether we realize it or not.

In meditating with others, your presence supports and helps everyone else – and theirs supports you. This is true whether you, or they, consciously realize it or not. This was pressed home to me one evening after I had been away for a few days. A friend came up to me after meditation and said half-jokingly, 'Steve, *I* don't have to be here every day, but *you* do.'

Meditating with others also opens us up to feeling the pain of others, as well as the pain of the world. Yet we don't personalize it. Thus, in meditation we learn to understand and to take on the pain of the world without succumbing to it or feeling crushed by it.

If you have the opportunity to meditate with a group, I strongly recommend it, ideally on a regular basis.

You'll recall from Chapter 7 that the Chinese character for sitting meditation depicts two people sitting on the Earth. Not one person, but two. Why? Because it's not possible to meditate as a separate ego.

Even if you're meditating alone at home, it's not really just you, alone, sitting in meditation. You're not something separate and apart from everything else that's taking place *now*, as *this moment*.

If you can't shake yourself of the notion that *you* do meditation, that's okay. Please go ahead and practice anyway. We all begin with this notion and feeling – but over time, with practice, you will come to know what meditation actually is, and your need to constantly make yourself the reference point by which everything else is measured will weaken and fall away. This is actually the ticket to true happiness.

13. No Judgment

We are always judging. We judge our meditation practice. We judge each other. We judge our circumstances. We judge ourselves. ('There I go, passing judgment again. I really need to stop.')

Whenever we judge, however, we are not *here*. We're completely out of the moment. We've splintered the world in our mind and set ourselves off from that other thing we're judging.

Sometimes we even set ourselves off from ourselves and then judge *that* as though it were an object. 'My mind just won't stop judging! It's driving me crazy.' We try to take hold of our own judging mind, thinking that somehow we can do something about it.

To deal with this problem, all we need to do is realize what we're doing and drop it – that is, come back to *here* and *now*.

In doing so, however, we need to go easy on ourselves. We allow ourselves to have a distracted, obsessive, judgmental mind, if that's what's coming up right now, and we straightforwardly acknowledge it for what it is. This is essential, for if we try to wrestle our judging mind to the ground or fight it off, we'll just feed it and keep the process going. We only strengthen our judgmental mind by judging ourselves, by judging our judging.

But if we just come back, look honestly at what we're doing, and let the judging go – if we learn to come back and come back and come back – eventually our judgmental mind will lose its strength. It may continue to muscle in at times, but if we learn not to try to control it or to take hold of it, we'll discover that it will gradually lose its grip.

When we *see* in this way, we can then move freely through the world, and we can settle down in meditation without being disturbed by our own mind.

14. Frog Sitting

Picture the life of a frog. It sits by the edge of a pond on a lily pad. The afternoon sun streams down and reflects off the surface of the water. Birds fly overhead; a few chirp in nearby trees. A squirrel scampers by, a dragonfly flits among the tall grasses along the pond's muddy bank.

Amid all this activity, the frog sits quietly.

Suddenly, in one swift movement, the frog extends his tongue and snatches a fly buzzing by.

The frog swallows, then resumes sitting quietly as before.

A cloud moves in. From it fall a few heavy drops of rain. One raindrop hits the frog square on the head. He blinks once and continues to sit quietly.

Can you sit in meditation like a frog?

Meditation has two aspects. On the one hand, we learn to settle down and become stable. On the other, we remain flexible and open. If we have to move, we do.

Thus we avoid both extremes. We're neither frozen in place, rigid and inflexible, nor do we react to each little thing that occurs. Meditation takes the middle way between these two extremes.

Meditation has to do with appropriate action, not inaction. If you realize your house is on fire, you don't just sit there; you respond!

As you learn to settle your mind and remain attentive, like the frog, it will become obvious when and how to act.

This is equally true for the frog. If he's inattentive or tuned out, when a fly lands nearby, he'll miss his lunch. If this keeps up, eventually he'll starve to death.

In meditation, you're aware and ready for *this moment* as it comes to be. When it's time to eat, eat. When it's time to work, work. When it's time for formal sitting meditation, sit.

The frog is aware of all the activity going on around him – but he's not caught up in it. He just sits there calmly. Like so, in meditation, we're aware of our surroundings, the position and feel of our body, and the activity of our mind.

When it's time to croak, croak. And when it's time to eat, eat. Except for our being bound in thought, *just sitting* couldn't be easier.

15. Stillness in Movement

The essence of meditation is stillness in the midst of activity.

Activity is essential to life. Nothing in this world stays still, even for a moment – not our thoughts, not our feelings, not our bodies. The physical world, both macroscopically and microscopically, is nothing but activity. So is our mental world much of the time.

In meditation, we discover very quickly just how busy our minds usually are. But, also in meditation, we have the opportunity to taste the stillness that is always *here* in the midst of unending movement and change.

This stillness in movement may seem like a contradiction, but it is actually quite common. For example, consider a hurricane. It has a still place at its center, around which turmoil circles. Yet even the eye of a hurricane doesn't stay put. In a hurricane, stillness and movement are thus inseparable.

Or consider a wheel turning around a hub. No matter how fast the wheel turns, the hub at its center remains still.

In meditation, we touch this stillness. We realize the very center of the turning wheel, the still point at the center of the world.

*

In the first of his *Four Quartets*, T. S. Eliot created multiple images of stillness in movement. He wrote of the Chinese jar that moves perpetually in its stillness.

Imagine this Chinese jar and the intricate and dynamic pattern painted on it. Looking at this pattern, this frozen image, we find movement.

As we imagine this jar, there is also movement in our minds. We are moved by the exquisite artistry, by the sweep and curve of its shape and patterns, and by its aged patina.

Stillness pervades it all, yet if we look more closely at the jar, on the molecular level, we find still more rapid movement. And at the quantum level, the jar is nothing but a blur of energy and flux, with nothing staying put anywhere.

The whole world is awash in such movement. Yet in meditation, we learn not to get caught up in that movement.

Reality is activity and stillness working together. The blur of energy and movement we don't see creates this manifest world that we do. Thus, stillness and movement are forever found in the same place at once. Yet it is only within stillness that we can appreciate this.

The activity of coming back to *here* and *now* is the return to stillness at the world's ever-present center.

16. It's Not About Getting Things Done

Meditation is not about throwing things out of your mind or trying to make your mind blank. For starters, this is impossible. If you try to throw things out of your mind, how will you throw out the final thing – the willful mind that has been busily throwing things out?

Meditation is not about doing anything. It is pure attention without grasping, without interference. It is simply paying attention.

If our will is directed toward any object or purpose – even toward meditating correctly – then we're not in meditation. We're doing something.

But isn't paying attention doing something? Actually, no – not if it is pure, simple attention devoid of hope, fear, dread, or expectation. Bare attention, in fact, is the only activity that does *not* involve doing something. (Indeed, even calling it an activity isn't accurate since meditation is neither active nor passive.)

None of this means, of course, that we should try to stop being active participants in our lives. That would be another impossibility. Indeed, trying to stop any activity is itself an activity. We can't stop acting. Life itself is never-ending action. The crux of the matter does not hinge on action, but on our will.

We can only act appropriately if we are *here*. If we're caught up in our ideas, hopes, fears, explanations, mental stories, or internal monologues, we'll act out of being all bound up in these rather than out of the situation at hand.

For instance, imagine that a young child is standing on the sidewalk, and suddenly runs into the street. If you're paying attention, you won't have to figure out what to do. You'll know how to act. Or, more accurately, you'll simply act and act appropriately without having any sense of knowing or not knowing what to do.

Meditation doesn't require that we become vegetables. Quite the opposite, it shows us how to wake up from our distracted and sometimes vegetative states of mind. It teaches us to be fully present with whatever activity we're doing, and to engage in it wholeheartedly.

When it's time to sit in meditation, just sit in meditation. When it's time to clean your house, clean house. When it's time to speak, speak. When it's time for silence, keep silent. It's very simple.

Meditation often seems difficult because it runs contrary to how we've been trained throughout our lives. We've been brought up to get things done rather than just to be present. In meditation, we stop clinging to that urge to do something that has been encouraged and bred in us for so long. We learn to experience life as a whole, without resorting to measure.

If we focus only on getting things done, the transience of life becomes burdensome. But if we slow down and attend to our life as it unfolds from moment to moment, we can taste how sweet life really is. We can appreciate the fleeting purples and pinks that fill the evening sky. We can appreciate the song of the cardinal as it stirs in late winter. We can love our children in all their rambunctious antics because we know they will not be children long. We can be grateful for friends and family, even when we do not agree with their views. And we can stop trying to find or acquire something other than what appears before us in *this moment*.

Meditation is continually returning to life so that we don't miss it. It's realizing that in *this moment* there's no doer and there's nothing to be done. It's the immediacy of mind, moment, and Reality. There's no gap, no distinction, between you and what you're doing.

Actually, this is how things always are in Reality. It's only in our concepts, and with our conceptual minds, that we separate ourselves from any activity. Then we make a judgment, labeling the activity good or bad. This is where we become bored with doing the dishes – or bored with life.

But our problem is not that our lives are boring; it's that we don't allow ourselves to live fully. We would never experience boredom or anxiety, unhappiness or depression, if we learned to be *here*. These afflictions only arise in a mind caught up in thought – and in the petty concerns of this little self.

Life is larger than our thoughts. The impermanence that appears in life continuously creates something new in each moment. If we just pay attention, we'll see that life is constantly showing us something fresh. Our task is to simply attend to what's taking place – and to act appropriately.

In meditation, we cultivate a mind that *just sees* rather than a mind that is caught up in doing and seeking and achieving.

In meditation, we *see* that experience is never divided. We *see* in each moment that there's nothing that has to be done apart from living in full Awareness. *Seeing* is immediate release – and it's as near as taking the next breath.

17. It Couldn't Be Simpler

Meditation is really very simple.

We don't appreciate this, however, because our minds are very complicated, and we bring much of that complicatedness to the practice of meditation.

We don't mean to, of course; in fact, we probably don't even realize that we do it. Yet we do it repeatedly, even habitually.

The Chinese Zen master Foyan often pointed out how we needlessly complicate things. He said, 'Why do you not understand your nature when it's inherently present? There's not much to the teaching of the awakened – it only requires getting to the essential. We don't teach that you annihilate random thoughts, suppress body and mind, and shut your eyes… Just observe your present state. What is the reason for it? Why do you become confused?'

Zen, meditation, enlightenment, awakening, Truth, Reality, Dharma – all of these things seem so vague and mysterious. But they are not. As Bodhidharma, who brought Zen from India to China, said, they're clear and obvious.

Truth is right *here*. Where else would you expect to experience it? Why do you feel you have to go off and do something special in order to gain understanding?

There's not much to the teaching of the awakened, as

Master Foyan said. Yes, there are many schools of Buddhism, and myriad practices, texts, and teachings that we can study and contemplate. Yes, these teachings are often subtle and profound. In the end, however, there's really not much to this matter. It only requires getting to the essential.

Yet somehow we find this immeasurably difficult. We don't take Master Foyan at his word and thus we complicate the matter. We ignore what he just pointed out and launch into thought. 'Yeah, getting to the essential, that's gotta be something! This is deep stuff.' What we mean by this, of course, is 'this is hard to figure out.'

We're lost right out of the gate. We've already departed from the simple teaching that was just pointed out to us.

We refuse to understand 'simple.'

Meditation really is simple. Very simple. I'm not using code here. It really, really is simple.

We take meditation practice, which is utterly simple, to be difficult because we don't really take it up. Instead of practicing *now* and *here*, we get lost in thought about it and then discuss what we think.

We do this not just with meditation practice, but with simplicity itself. We hold tight to the package we've labeled 'simple,' not noticing that we've mentally turned it into a sticky ball of vagueness and complexity that we can't easily let go of. And then we're lost in confusion.

But waking up *is* very simple. It's *right now*. Enlightenment is not something removed from you, a particular thing you have to get. It's not something to get an idea of or to figure out. In fact, it can't be figured out.

Nor is enlightenment something hard to experience. You're experiencing it *right now*, though you may be ignoring the experience.

Just pause for a moment and recall your state of mind when you read the previous sentence – that you're already experiencing enlightenment but ignoring it. Did you instantly lunge into mental complexity, into thought? Did you try to figure out what I meant, or how what I said could be true, or how you could possibly ignore your own experience?

This is what you need to start noticing if you would awaken. Start noticing how quickly you grasp at things, how you make complex what is inherently simple.

Let go of trying to figure it out.

If you would realize and understand Reality, you must look at your mind *now*.

Unexamined, your mind quickly becomes very complicated. It's grasping, reaching, trying to take hold of something and reel it in. But that 'something' isn't *here*.

When you're caught up in thought, you're somewhere else – off in the future, lost in the past, or enveloped in fantasy.

The awakened are always up-front about this. 'It's right *here!* Why are you confused?'

People often think meditation is about driving thoughts out of your mind. But this isn't meditation at all, as Foyan correctly points out. You don't need to annihilate thoughts. Thoughts annihilate themselves, if you'll let them. They simply fall apart. Everything does.

Yet we think we have to make an effort to drive them out. We don't realize that, in doing so, we only solidify them, and thus deepen our confusion and entanglement.

In Zen we don't teach people to annihilate their thoughts. Instead we sit quietly and learn to pay attention to what's actually happening. Thoughts will naturally drop away if you don't hang on to them, don't build them into something.

In another passage, Master Foyan points out, 'As soon as you rationalize, it's hard to understand Zen. You have to stop rationalizing before you will get it.' Astutely, he adds, 'Some people hear this kind of talk and say there is nothing to say and no reason – they do not realize they are already rationalizing.'

We make meditation difficult when we rationalize, when we explain, when we try to figure it out, when we start adding things. In doing so, we imagine what is not there and miss what is. And we don't recognize this as our continuous, ongoing delusion.

We only need to stop talking to ourselves and pay attention. Just notice what you're doing. Notice the grasping in your mind. Notice the reaching. Notice the endless lack of satisfaction. Notice your rationalizing as you rationalize, your searching as you search, and your grasping as you grasp.

Only when we stop grasping can we *see* our true nature.

Enlightenment isn't something we need to figure out. It's just remembering – waking up to what you *knew* all along but were not paying attention to. There's nothing complex or mysterious about it. It doesn't involve rockets going off in your head or trumpets blaring from the clouds. It's *just this*, but you're no longer confused about it.

There's nothing to figure out. It's only a matter of *seeing* and not talking to yourself.

Even as you read this, notice what your mind is doing.

18. Zero or 100%

By now I hope you realize that this book is not about getting the right *ideas* about meditation. This book is about taking it up and doing it.

As you become more familiar with the practice of meditation, you will begin to see for yourself that the instructions in this book don't operate in the usual 'effort in, results out' way, but in a much more subtle and less linear fashion.

In fact, strictly speaking, over time you'll discover that meditation won't give you ideas at all. It doesn't teach in that way. Rather, in meditation you will realize your own mind directly, and *see* for yourself just what is taking place *here* and *now*.

As a result, discussing meditation in a book necessarily involves making statements that, at first blush, might appear contradictory or paradoxical.

For example, as we become more intimate with meditation, we simultaneously learn to live the Middle Way and to take up each thing that we do 100 percent or else not take it up at all.

On the surface, these two aspects of meditation appear to contradict one another; in fact, however, they are inseparable, and manifest together naturally in each moment of awareness.

The 'Middle Way' is a term coined by the Buddha that refers to the avoidance of extremes. Rather than having a specific, narrow focus, such as going into a trance, or improving your health, or transporting yourself to some other realm, meditation is a broad, expansive awareness that leaves nothing out.

The 'Middle Way' also refers to this same non-specific, objectless Awareness.

The first time the Buddha used this term, it referred to avoiding the extremes of luxury and austerity, of indulgence and deprivation. But the 'Middle Way' shows up again and again in meditation, in many different ways. With practice, you will experience this for yourself. Eventually you will *see* that even existence and non-existence, and 'me' and 'everything that is not me,' are forms of extremes. You will *see* that these are ideas that do not match Reality.

At the same time, however, we should also realize that meditation is a matter of zero or 100 percent. Either you're present or you're not. There are no in-betweens.

There's no tiptoeing or gently lowering yourself into meditation, either. There's only jumping right in. It's not possible to mediate halfheartedly, haphazardly, or halfway. If you're half-engaged, you're not in meditation. There is no 'meditation lite.'

As my own teacher used to say, 'Zen is zero or 100 percent.' What he was talking about was wholeheartedness. This means giving our full attention to each thing we do, without holding back. It means not multitasking. It means experiencing each moment fully, whether it's pleasant or unpleasant, joyous or painful.

That's the 100 percent part. The zero part is the flip side. If you're only willing to meditate (or, really, do anything) halfheartedly or half-interestedly, it's better not to do it at all. Either cook dinner or don't. You wouldn't bake a soufflé halfway and serve it. If you want to adopt a pet, don't care for it only when you feel like it; either care for your pet wholeheartedly or don't take on the responsibility at all.

And if you want to wake up, don't think this is about coming back to *here* and *now* only when your life is running smoothly and you're feeling happy and relaxed – or only when you're feeling down and need an emotional pick-me-up.

We live in a time and a culture that reward 'getting things done' and multitasking. But following these cultural messages makes our lives needlessly complicated and difficult. We end up doing things halfheartedly – or at least part-heartedly. Instead of paying attention, we trade quality for quantity.

In meditation, we do exactly the opposite. We pay attention wholeheartedly without attempting to do anything or get anything done or make anything right.

It's rare for most of us to focus on a single task, to settle into the present, to really be *here*, to soak into this precious, fleeting moment 100 percent. But we can do this if we decide to. Indeed, we *need* to do it if we are to wake up to what each moment actually presents.

A big part of doing things 100 percent – and of the Middle Way – thus involves saying no. It means refusing to do too many things, even when everyone around you is. It means not multitasking except when you absolutely have to (for instance, if you're caring for young children). It means not driving yourself crazy with innumerable tasks and responsibilities. It even means, occasionally, accomplishing nothing at all.

Notice how such choices at once represent both zero and 100 percent – and how they walk a Middle Way between franticness and laziness, and between over-responsibility and irresponsibility.

To the extent that we're not fully present as we live our life, a good portion of our life passes away unlived. It slips right past us and we do not taste it.

This matter of zero or 100 percent has to do with your own mind, your own attitude, and your approach to life. If you are interested in awakening in each moment, you have to take up each moment wholeheartedly. This is what we do in meditation.

Perhaps when you're on the job, you have no choice but to multitask. If this is your situation, then it's very helpful to realize it. (Just remember that you're not really a computer, and that what we call multitasking is really task switching. The fact is, high-speed computer or not, we can only do one thing at a time.) And when it's time to stop your multitasking, then stop it at 100 percent (which, of course, equals zero).

This is meditation practice – coming to life in the only place you can: *here* and *now*.

Meditation can't be rushed or postponed. In fact, you can't do anything with it. As soon as you try to do something with it (or to it, or about it), you're not meditating. This is what makes meditation unique. This is what makes meditation meditation. There is no finish line in meditation. There's never a time when you graduate and are done with it.

Perhaps you've heard the common – and commonly misunderstood – analogy about a raft. The Buddha explained that if we're on one side of the river and want to get to the other, a raft would be very helpful. But once we're across, we need to leave the raft behind. Trying to drag it with us as we continue our journey overland will only burden us needlessly.

People often misunderstand this analogy. They sometimes think that meditation is the raft he was talking about that can take them to the other shore, and that can and should eventually be abandoned. *In fact, meditation is precisely the opposite.* It takes us nowhere. Instead, it brings us back to where we already are, over and over and over. Unlike everything else we do – and everything we think about – meditation *doesn't* take us somewhere else.

The raft that we use temporarily and then leave behind is not meditation, but things like this book. We would read about meditation rather than do it. The raft is helpful, of course, but the tasting is in the eating and not in the study of recipes. To the extent we don't take it up 100 percent, though we may be charmed and entertained by our reading, talking, thinking, and even dabbling in meditation, we will not taste life fully or live *this moment* wholeheartedly – which is precisely what meditation is.

Meditation requires regular time, attention, and commitment. Either commit to it and do it regularly, or forget about it and do something else instead. Meditating twice a month, or in spurts, or whenever you feel like it isn't meditation. It's dabbling. You can't dabble in meditation any more than you can dabble in breathing or eating or sleeping.

But what if you simply don't have time for meditation in your life right now? This may appear to be a legitimate issue, but resolving it means looking at your life and quite possibly letting go of something else (or even several things).

You have to make this choice yourself; no one else can do it for you. The result will be that you do fewer things – but, as you learn to be present, you will experience and likely enjoy each of those things far more. By removing some things from your life – by taking them to zero – you open up an opportunity to live life 100 percent.

19. Beyond Sitting Cross-Legged

It has been observed that it's important to learn all the rules so you can break them properly.[3] Yet it's also important not to stray too far from the heart of meditation by getting lost in details.

In meditation, you needn't stay within the lines – but it's wise to never lose sight of them, either.

We must walk a middle path between a practice that is too loose or sloppy and one that is rigid and righteous. As the calligraphy master tells students, 'Be loose with the brush.' Let us be at once flexible and playful, yet disciplined; loose and at ease, yet attentive.

While there are many wrong ways to meditate – for example, while watching a sitcom on television – there's no one 'right' way. Indeed, meditation isn't about doing things correctly.

Meditation is awareness. So, if the 'right' way to enter the meditation hall is left foot first, but you mistakenly enter with your right foot instead, just be aware of how you *are* entering. Never mind what's 'right.'

In time, as you learn to observe your own mind, gradually you'll realize the details of meditation practice, and doing everything in the 'proper' way will follow naturally.

---

[3] This aphorism is often attributed to the Dalai Lama. In fact, it comes from *Life's Little Instruction Book*, by H. Jackson Brown, Jr. (Nashville, Tenn.: Rutledge Hill, 1991).

So don't worry about the details. Indeed, when you fixate on doing meditation 'right' or worry about doing it 'wrong,' you aren't meditating.

It is far better to step out of that kind of narrow practice – out of the mental cross-legged posture into which we can become bound. Just realize that meditation is much more than doing things in a particular way.

Some people employ the meditative practice of prayers, or *gathas*. These are short verses that people regularly recite – either aloud or to themselves – on all kinds of occasions. They're little verbal or mental reminders that can help you draw your attention to the activity at hand, or to slow yourself down and return to the present moment. For example, you might recite a *gatha* before you eat, or brush your teeth, or pick up the phone. As an aid to drawing your attention to your own state of mind, reciting *gathas* can be a wonderful practice.

But there's also a danger. You can load up your life with verses until you can't make a move without saying something to yourself. Reciting *gathas* ceases to be a ritual practice of awareness and becomes instead a mindless habit. So take care not to take up too much. If a practice begins to clutter your mind, simplify or get rid of it. This, of course, applies to any practice, not just reciting verses.

With meditation, 'less is more' is especially true.

Meditation isn't about holding on to any particular form – yet it can't be done without form, either.

In meditation, we need to begin with some basic rules

and guidelines. Yet, over time, all the rules and guidelines, all the rights and wrongs, all the 'shoulds' and 'shouldn'ts' drop away. We let go of doing meditation 'right.'

Eventually we even let go of 'doing meditation' and of 'letting go.' The mind settles naturally into itself.

20. Slowing Down

Many of us feel rushed much of the time, if not outright frantic. We race about, doing this and looking for that. Life keeps accelerating, and we so easily get caught up in it.

So it might seem that a book on meditation would include tips to help you slow things down in your life.

Not this book, though. In fact, trying to slow things down will only make matters worse, and make you even more frustrated.

The truth is that we really can't slow things down – at least, not 'out there' in the world. There *is* something we can do to correct the problem – something quite direct and immediate. But it's not applied where most of us think it needs to be.

We often unwittingly fight with meditation – the very thing we expect will put us at peace – because we get stuck in our desire to slow things down. This desire (which we often conceive of as a need) creates an antagonistic approach to the hurly-burly of life. There's us here and the pace of life over there, and we believe it's our job to wrestle life to the ground and hold it still, or at least calm it down.

But as we take up meditation, the hurly-burly of life needn't be our concern at all. We don't need to try to control what's happening 'out there,' because, for the most part, we can't!

The world won't be stopped, or even slowed down. There's no way to put the brakes on it. It keeps rolling along, and as long as you view your problem as 'out there,' and want to control it or fix it or slow it down, you'll needlessly frustrate yourself. You'll continue to feel hurried, confused, and unsettled – the very opposite of what you're looking for.

So stop looking for it.

In taking up meditation we do something quite different. First we start to notice how anything 'out there' – whatever it is – so easily captures us. Then we also notice that, once we're captured, we're no longer *here*.

In meditation, we take careful note of what is taking place right *here*. We don't comment on any of it. We just tune in. If our mind is carrying on about how fast and terrible the pace of life has become, then we simply notice that internal rant, without judging it or trying to do anything about it.

When we first take up meditation, most of us are astounded when we discover just how agitated, noisy, and insanely busy our minds are. If we were to actually verbalize all the inane chatter of our mind, others would think us crazy.

And when we sit in meditation even for only a few minutes, following our breath, we soon notice something else: everything that bothers us about the rapid pace of life 'out there' is, in fact, true of our own mind. It quickly becomes clear that we're not *here* very often.

We tell ourselves that our problem is all that stuff 'out there.' 'My job drives me to distraction.' 'My neighbor is noisy.' 'This country is going downhill.' 'I just want to slow down, but with my partner it's always go, go, go.' It's this. It's that. We latch on to something 'out there' and let it carry us away from what is actually going on *here*. But it's *here* where we need to take care of the problem.

Once we start noticing how busy our mind is most of the time, it can sometimes seem like there's not much distinguishing the busyness and craziness of the world 'out there' from what's going on in our own mind. Yet our mind is just where we need to look.

If you look at a weather map, you'll usually see highs and lows. If the map has only one high or low, and the isobars (the lines demarking places of equal pressure) are spaced far apart across the map, you are generally looking at very calm, stable weather. But if the map has a lot of highs and lows on it, you're looking at windy conditions.

When a high-pressure cell and a low-pressure cell come into close proximity, the isobars move closer and closer together. When this happens, the wind speeds pick up. There's a lot of activity, a lot of rushing about.

When we feel a lot of mental wind rushing through our mind, it's analogous to a weather map where the isobars are close together. Many highs and lows come and go and move around. All is in constant flux. There's a lot of windy, gusty, turbulent mental weather.

In fact, any time we have a distinct idea, belief, or opinion about 'this' that's set off against 'that,' there will be movement in our mind. Once we've created something distinct, solid, separate, and removed from ourselves, there will be a lot of chasing and rushing about.

But all this agitation is only in your mind.

In meditation we learn not to get caught up in this agitation – or in our thoughts, or in the world. We let things, thoughts, feelings, and images arise, flash past, and dissipate like mist in the sun.

With meditation the highs and lows of our mind begin to die down, spread out, and move apart, even though the world 'out there' keeps rolling on.

Ultimately we come to realize that the very distinction of 'out there' and 'in here' is just another mental construct. It isn't Real. The distinction of 'me' – I'm removed from that, I'm watching that, I'm driven by that, I'm related to that – dies down as it's realized that what's actually experienced is always *here*. There is no 'out there' or 'in here.' There's just *here, now*.

'All right,' you may say. 'So I can't slow down the world. But I can slow myself down, can't I? Isn't that a good thing?'

Not necessarily. Consider, once again, the child about to dash into the street. It's time to move quickly.

Some events naturally occur at a rapid pace. Often, we'll need to match that pace. But we don't need to feel rushed just because things around us are unfolding at high speed. If we *see* what's going on, we don't have to rush, but can simply be present. At whatever pace things unfold, we unfold with them. We don't need to be hurried or flustered or frustrated or driven – even if we're moving very fast. We just relax into what's unfolding, realizing that there's nothing we need to chase after or keep pace with.

As long as you know that none of it is ultimately substantial, you don't need to be flustered. You can be right there with it. If you feel you're being rushed at work, just bring your mind into the moment – into the task at hand – and you won't feel rushed, even if you've got to work fast.

People who are in an auto accident often report that the crash seemed to unfold in slow motion. They saw the windshield shattering, the individual shards of glass tumbling through the air. Many details of the event are etched into their minds, as if the event was prolonged and they had time to study it. And yet, to bystanders witnessing the crash, it all happened in a split second.

Why? Because in that very brief time, the person in the accident was really *there* – fully present. They weren't distracted by thought.

When we awaken into *this moment*, we experience this same effect. Nothing is actually slowed, of course – but our attention has sharpened, allowing us to better see it all unfold.

The more present we are, the bigger the picture we see. The bigger the picture we see, the more things seem to slow down. And when the Whole is *seen*, all is utterly still.

21. An Honest Question

Once you've taken up meditation – particularly if you encounter Zen – you may hear the expression 'Meditation is useless.'

This is troubling, or at least puzzling, for people new to meditation. And it can be bothersome to even those who are not so new. A friend who has practiced meditation for a number of years recently told me that she felt it would be disingenuous of her to say that she practices meditation for no reason.

It's good that she's honest. If you do meditate for a reason, it's best that you admit it to yourself. If you are really to take up this practice, it's imperative that you be completely honest with yourself.

But why *should* we meditate for no reason? How can we continue with any activity if we don't think we'll get something from it?

The twentieth-century Zen teacher Shunryu Suzuki encouraged people to meditate with 'no gaining idea.' This phrase penetrates to the very heart and mind of an awakened person. It also points to something profound in human life that we usually miss, but which points to liberation.

Almost everything we do is done for a purpose, a result, an outcome. We do A in order to bring about B.

In meditation, however, we let go of hopes and fears, plans and outcomes, and simply come back to *here* and *now*.

This means that if we meditate in order to create any results – even in order to come back to *here* and *now* – we're not actually meditating. That is, we're not actually *here* and *now* but lost in the thought of coming back to *here* and *now*.

It's true that the awakened practice meditation with no sense of gain. But then they do everything with no sense of gain. That's how they hoe the garden or take out the garbage. They just hoe or carry – completely, totally, with no time or energy going into extraneous thoughts. There's no longing or loathing in the heart, no expectation or dread or hope of what will come of it. They're simply fully present.

The enlightened mind remains forever *here*, in whatever is taking place *now*, in this very moment. It's not wanting to change things, or wanting to be somewhere else other than *here*, or allowing itself to be carried off by ideas of doing *this* for some other purpose.

So maybe you do have some 'gaining ideas' about meditation. Whether it's right or wrong, you do want to calm down, or get enlightened, or *see* Truth.

If this is so in your case, then just realize it. Don't get down on yourself about it. In fact, it's normal and natural to have such expectations and justifications, especially at first. Why should we expect ourselves to understand right off what the awakened realize?

In fact, at the beginning, it's enough just to hear that

the awakened meditate without goals or expectations, and that we don't scoff at the idea, or at them for doing it. Yet, as we reflect on this, we'll gradually come to see something subtle and profound about it.

Some people wrestle with this for awhile, then tell themselves, 'It's no use; I can't help myself. I want meditation to make me happier, or a better person, or enlightened. I'm just a greedy, grasping, selfish person at heart. I'll never be able to meditate without wanting something from it. I might as well quit.'

But this is not the time to quit. These kinds of thoughts indicate that you're being honest with yourself. Keep at it, and keep being honest. Don't try to transcend your desire for gain. That's just another desire.

So what if you're greedy and grasping at this moment? You can still let it go. Just be who you are – which is nothing in particular. In other words, just because you're grasping or selfish in one moment doesn't mean you're destined to be so in the next. Every moment is a fresh opportunity, a world born anew.

This is not to say that there are no benefits to meditation. There may be many. But in meditation, we let go of all cost/benefit thinking.

This isn't as strange as it sounds. For example, there are many benefits to eating. But do we really need to consider or enumerate them? Do we need to give ourselves good reasons to eat? Or is it enough simply to eat?

*

Look at what this issue of meditating for no reason is pointing to. Don't try to grasp anything. If you take hold of it, it won't make any sense. But if you look at it without trying to grasp it, it could be wisdom.

In order to realize the more profound aspects of meditation, when you *do* encounter something about it that doesn't make sense to you, don't just ignore it or leave. Sit with it. Reflect on it. Come back to it once in a while. Digest it. It will eventually penetrate your mind and heart – and it may start to heat up, or even burn. That's good. Just continue to sit with it. Let the thought of 'nothing to gain' come back to you. Don't tell yourself you understand it if you don't yet. But when you *do see* for yourself, you will taste true freedom of mind.

Here's yet another way to look at this. Imagine a spaceship on its launchpad ready to send a group of astronauts into orbit. Their tiny capsule sits atop enormous booster rockets that fire up and lift an entire assemblage of rockets and payload into the thin upper reaches of the atmosphere. But the huge, weighty boosters have to drop away before the next stage rockets kick in, or their enormous weight will pull everything back to Earth.

We come to meditation with a lot of misguided ideas that motivate us to take up the practice in the first place. These motives and ideas are the 'big boosters' that get us started. But once we're on our way, clearing the atmosphere and heading for orbit, those same motives and ideas have to go, or they will become a weight that will pull us down.

There will come a point in your own meditation practice when you're no longer telling yourself anything about what you're doing or why. This, too, is normal and natural. Simply stay with the practice. You have to give up, but don't stop.

Eventually, as you continue to practice, you'll enter a place where there's nothing supporting you in your efforts. It's critical at this stage to let thoughts of gain and benefit drop away. Just stay with it. If your effort is consistently on returning to *here* and *now* and nothing more, liberation will already be realized.

If you look very carefully at anything you can grasp – no matter how sound it may appear in your hand or mind, or how desperately you may feel you need it – it will start to unravel, and eventually fall apart. This is why the world appears so enigmatic, paradoxical, strange, and contradictory to us when we seriously contemplate it.

But meditation practiced for no reason and for no gain will *not* unravel or fall apart. Instead, it will show us what is beyond our grasp.

22. Collecting the Mind

What is sesshin? Sesshin, originally a Japanese word, now also used in English, means to collect the mind. It's not our ordinary activity. It could be, but usually it's not. Usually we're very scattered. It may never occur to us to collect the mind. At Zen centers, blocks of time are commonly set aside each year for this activity.

To keep things simple, in this chapter I'll use the word sesshin rather than some awkward contrivance since there is no other word for this activity in English.

Sometimes people refer to sesshin as a 'meditation retreat,' yet it's anything but a retreat. A retreat is a step away from the world, a chance to distance ourselves from everyday reality for a time. But a sesshin is quite the opposite: it's stepping *into* Reality – that is, it's to bring ourselves back to *this moment*, over and over and over for a period usually lasting several days.

Since there is no one right way to conduct a sesshin (indeed, since there are different kinds of sesshins), what is described here is merely typical of sesshins and is neither required by nor exhaustive of all sesshins.

In a typical sesshin, we limit our activities to sitting, walking, eating, sleeping, and sometimes working (usually for a brief period each day). Very often the sesshin leader or teacher will give a talk each day, as well. We slow down and settle into the moment, so that these activities become sitting meditation, eating meditation, listening meditation, working meditation, and so on.

All of this is done according to a schedule, though that schedule doesn't necessarily need to be posted or memorized in advance. A simple sequence of bells usually tells participants when to enter the meditation hall, when to get up, when to walk, when to stop working, and so on. No one needs a watch. A sesshin thus gives us the opportunity not to be caught by time.

In a typical sesshin there is no reading, or napping, or talking (except for possible interviews with the teacher or any brief, necessary exchange of words during work periods). Except when necessary, eye contact is avoided. Meals are served and eaten in silence in the meditation hall. There are typically short breaks after each meal. Often during a mid-afternoon break, tea or coffee and a treat are served.

Though what I just described may be typical, there are variations in sesshins from teacher to teacher and from meditation group to meditation group. Kosho Uchiyama, a Japanese meditation teacher, recently deceased, who is known by many in the United States through his books, led sesshins that included no lectures and no work. There were only four activities: sitting meditation, walking meditation, eating meditation, and sleeping meditation.

In sesshin, we have the opportunity to drop our own egos, preferences, and ways of doing things. Everything is very simple and focused. There's nothing we need to think about or worry about. We simply do what needs to be done in each moment – nothing more.

In sesshin, nothing competes with anything else. Everything is reduced to the essentials, yet comes together as a Whole. Sesshin provides an opportunity for all participants to serve one another and be served.

Why participate in a sesshin? Without giving specific reasons, since doing meditation for any purpose is a contradiction in terms, sesshin offers us a unique experience that can't easily be found in any other situation.

For most of us, during our first years (or decades) of meditation practice, we meditate intermittently during our official meditation times, then go back to our usual mind – a mind of getting and seeking, of longing and loathing, of spinning stories to ourselves – for most of the rest of each day. It usually takes a very long time for meditation to soak fully into our life, and for us to learn to come back to *here* and *now* in any situation, whether we're formally meditating or not.

Sesshin gives us a chance to taste this mind of ongoing, undivided attention. In sesshin, we don't stop meditating when the bell rings, or when we leave the meditation hall, or when we go to sleep at night.

My meditation teacher once told me, 'Sesshin is necessary for the long run.' In other words, if you're going to take up meditation for life, you need to experience sesshin. Ultimately, meditation can't just be a component of our life. It must become a way of life – or, more accurately, life itself. After all, we're only truly living when we're *here*.

In sesshin, we live life fully. Not that this can't occur outside of sesshin, but in sesshin we remove excessive distractions for prolonged periods. We also gain the support of others around us who are making this same effort. In sesshin we're encouraged not to turn off our awareness after thirty or forty or eighty minutes simply because, at least for a time, we don't have to go back to our everyday distractions and our everyday distracted mind. This is yet another way in which we collect the mind.

Ordinarily our day-to-day activity is filled with 'things I like,' 'things I don't like,' 'things that are fun,' 'things that are not fun,' 'things that are important,' 'things that are not important,' and so on. We bring this sort of attitude to everything we do, trying to pick and choose, and doing our best to alter our circumstances to match our preferences. But in sesshin we don't carry on this way. We just do what we're called on to do, regardless of what we may think, or feel, or prefer.

In collecting the mind, we don't compartmentalize the activity of the moment. Rather, we *see* how everything functions together as a Whole, and we carry out our activities accordingly.

During a work period at a sesshin, for example, if you're assigned a task, the point is not to get it done as quickly as possible and then move on to the next thing. In meditation, the purpose of the task is to do the task – completely and thoroughly, without extraneous thought.

If you think of a sesshin as elapsing in time, you may find it difficult to get through it. To the extent that you remain caught in time, you may feel impatient or frustrated. Just settle into the sesshin and forget about time altogether.

It's not unusual, on the first day of sesshin, that the mind is busily chasing about. This agitated mind can be annoying and perhaps even maddening to us. But by the second or third day of sesshin, the mind may begin to settle into *this moment*, and difficulty and mental discomfort will fall away.

In the early days of our meditation center, we held a number of one-day sesshins because we weren't set up to have longer ones. People wound up believing that longer sesshins would consist of day after day of frantic mental activity. After we were able to do longer sesshins, however, we eventually eliminated the one-day ones, because they gave people the impression that longer *sesshins* would be impossibly difficult.

It's very much like the difference between a short and a long road trip. Before we opened our meditation center here in Minneapolis, I occasionally drove to Eau Claire, Wisconsin, 100 miles away, to give workshops or lead sesshins there. The drive always seemed long enough, and I'd often arrive feeling a little road-weary. I was grateful that it wasn't any farther.

As I was getting used to the regular drive to Eau Claire, however, I had occasion to drive to Chicago, which is 300 miles beyond Eau Claire. On that drive, as I passed by the freeway exit I took on my trips to Eau Claire, I felt like I had only just begun my journey. I still had plenty of stamina to continue on to Chicago. In fact, I felt like I had barely left home. The reason, of course, was that I was psyched up to drive much farther.

It works the same way with sesshins. If all you know is

a one-day *sesshin*, you will likely reach the end of that day and think, 'This is long enough. I couldn't possibly sit a two-day, let alone a five- or seven-day sesshin.' But in sesshin, the second day is not at all like the first day, or the third day like the second, and so on. As the days pass, the mind stops resisting and begins to settle into *here* and *now*.

In sesshin, eating is much more than chowing down. Before we begin, we pause to reflect on the fact that we eat not only to support our life, but in the context of this integrated Whole which is the sesshin and, indeed, the world itself. We consider the life of what we are about to eat. We also acknowledge the labors of the many people who produced, transported, and prepared our food and served it to us.

As we eat, we bring our attention back, over and over, to the full taste and texture and color of the food, the weight and feel of the bowl in our hand, and so on. We drop any evaluation of the food and, indeed, any thought about it. We just eat. We eat wholeheartedly.

All of us like certain foods more than others, but sesshin provides us with the opportunity to let all that go. This is not a time to indulge our personal preferences. We have plenty of opportunity for that elsewhere. If a food that you're not particularly fond of is being served, so what? Life always dishes up some things we don't like. Here's an opportunity to partake of something you don't usually enjoy without getting upset about it. (By the same token, don't go overboard when it happens to be something you like, either.)

Unless what's being served would make you ill (for example, if you're seriously allergic to it), take at least a little. If it's merely something that doesn't agree with you – say it's cucumbers – just take a small portion in the spirit of gratitude.

Again, by the same token, don't start loading up just because it's something you like. Remember, you're eating in the context of others. Just take what you need and no more.

Now a few words about physical pain in sesshin.

Sometimes people scare themselves away from sesshin with their own expectations of severe physical pain. They imagine terribly sore knees and ankles, stiff backs and necks, throbbing shoulders, and so on. Because they feel mildly (or more than mildly) uncomfortable after sitting in meditation for thirty or forty minutes, they imagine that sesshin will be physically excruciating. Sometimes these fears are confirmed by participants of previous sesshins who relish discussing their own intense physical pain. (More about these folks in a minute.)

Here's an important message on the subject: sesshin is not an endurance contest. You get no points for creating and enduring your own physical hell. (Remember that with meditation you get no points for anything.)

It's important for us to learn not to run from discomfort. In sesshin, just as we can learn to not resist tasks and to eat foods we would ordinarily avoid, we can also learn to not resist a certain amount of physical discomfort.

But there's a big difference between moderate discomfort and real pain. You already know how to sense when your body has crossed this line.

In sesshin, listen to your body. Once you've crossed over from discomfort to serious pain, make an adjustment. For the next meditation period, sit in a different position, or add a second cushion atop the first, or sit in a chair. There's no shame in this; in fact, there's wisdom and compassion in it.

There are those who feel that sitting in a chair is for wimps, that *real* meditators will just accept intense pain and tough it out for the entire sesshin. People who think this way cause themselves (and often lead others into) much needless stress, and even injury in some instances. As my meditation teacher put it, it's not necessary to commit suicide over meditation. It's imperative that you don't baby yourself (or expect others to), but do take care of yourself.

Look back at the guidelines on pain in Chapter 6. These apply to sesshin just as much as they do to everyday sitting. Please read those guidelines again, and be wise and compassionate enough with yourself to follow them in sesshin.

Usually we enjoy the sound of cicadas and the chirping of birds, but the lawnmower is unpleasant to our ears. We don't care to hear the jet plane flying overhead or the neighbor's barking dog. Sesshin gives us a wonderful opportunity to settle with all of it, no matter what is happening. We resist none of what we experience – not the food, not the work, not the sounds, not the heat or the cold. Not even the meditation itself.

In sesshin we have the perfect circumstance to ride it all out. We don't need to do anything about the jet or the dog or the lawnmower. We can let go of trying to arrange things to match our preferences and wants and cravings. We can attend to and stay with what is happening, no matter what we feel or think.

Sesshin is thus a precious opportunity to live free from our petty selves.

23. Sticky Sitting

Zen master Dahui said that the quickest way to get stuck in meditation is to look for a shortcut. He said, 'When you have even a single thought about looking for a shortcut in Zen, you have already stuck your head in a bowl of glue.'

Years ago, when I was a young Zen student, a friend who was also new to the practice grew discouraged at what appeared to be a long road ahead. He didn't seem to be getting anywhere. He told me he was thinking of going off to check out another teacher – not a Zen teacher, but someone from a different tradition altogether. When I asked him why, he told me that he thought it might be quicker.

That was over thirty years ago, and he's still looking.

But our teacher never promised us that we'd get somewhere. How could he? We can't get to somewhere else because there's nowhere else to get to. We're already *here*.

At first this seems discouraging to us. But it's only discouraging as long as we hold to the notion that life is about someplace other than where we are. Once it begins to dawn on us that we can never get anywhere other than *here*, everything in our approach to practice changes. For the first time the fresh oxygen of true freedom begins to sharpen our minds.

I teach a yearlong course on the great Buddhist teacher Nagarjuna. It's not an easy course. And I once had a student who, after studying a little bit of Nagarjuna with me, asked if he could test out of the class. I can sympathize with someone wanting to bypass Nagarjuna. He was one of the most profound writers from any culture, Eastern or Western, and he's very difficult to penetrate. But this is precisely why one does not test out of such things. It would be like testing out of life.

You don't test out of meditation, either. You don't arrive at a point where you can check it off your list. 'Task completed – I'm done.' What is this supposed to mean? That you've finally learned to meditate correctly and now you've graduated?

No. Meditation is about entering *this moment*. It's about waking to *this moment* again and again. We can't grasp *this*. And in the very realizing that *this* can't be gotten hold of, we are awake.

Grasping and acquisitiveness are very strong in most of us. This is not a recent development. Indeed, Master Dahui observed centuries ago, 'Many people today study meditation acquisitively.'

'But how else can we take it up?' we might ask. 'If it's not to get something, what's the point? Why else would we do it?'

Over and over again, Master Dahui – and others who

have awakened from confusion – tell us to just take up the practice wholeheartedly, without any calculations or thoughts of what we might get from it.

Master Dahui also adds, 'Just make your mind free.' But how are we supposed to do that when, as soon as he tells us that, we grasp? 'Oh yes, I want to make my mind free. What can I do right now to make my mind free?'

We have to have this pointed out to us over and over and over again in a myriad of ways. Just take a moment and look at your mind, even *now*. Notice the grasping, right there in that very approach that seeks to get an idea of what Dahui is saying.

We make our mind free not by grasping at something to make it free. We make it free by realizing it's already free, and by realizing that we've been grasping fruitlessly and unnecessarily. In short, we 'make it free' by not putting it in bondage in the first place.

For this, Master Dahui advises us not to be too tense or too loose. Don't hold to anything too tightly, but at the same time don't be wishy-washy, going whichever way the wind blows.

'Neither too tense nor too loose,' says Master Dahui, 'will save you mental energy,' because there's nothing to figure out. We burn up a lot of mental energy by grasping, but we can learn that we simply don't need to grasp.

When we approach meditation with our usual acquisitive mind, trying to take hold of one thing or another – enlightenment, tranquility, patience, awakening, wisdom – we'll only remain stuck.

And though it's pointed out repeatedly that enlightenment cannot be grasped or owned, still we objectify it. We set ourselves apart from it and then wonder how we can get our hands on it.

And then we wonder what it means when we're told that enlightenment cannot be grasped, because we interpret everything through our grasping, conceptualizing mind. We're nonplussed when we hear that enlightenment is already ours. We refuse to trust it.

But there's nothing confusing *here*. *This* is Reality. What need is there to grasp it? How could you, or anything else, ever be set apart from it?

When the Buddha, Nagarjuna, Dogen, and many others spoke of right intention in numerous ways, they were speaking of the pure desire to simply be awake, *now* and again *now* and again *now*, in each moment. The desire of one who is awake is simply to be awake.

It's not that the awakened have gotten hold of the right idea. They haven't gotten hold of anything. Instead, they have the right intention.

The intention of a buddha (one who is awake) is simply to be awake – an intention that's renewed in each moment. The awakened keep coming back to *just this*.

You must learn to look honestly and unflinchingly at your grasping mind. You must become aware that your mind says things like, 'I am going to do *this* so that I can get *that*.' Yet nothing intimately satisfies this acquisitive mind. Thus you get caught in a pattern of disappointment, and get your head stuck in a bowl of glue.

To the extent that we see things 'out there,' we'll try to

grasp them. But when it's truly understood that there's no essence to be distilled, and nothing to be gotten hold of, then there's no need to grasp. And when grasping falls away, awakening remains unshackled by thought.

24. Weather Watch

Meditation isn't about cutting off our feelings, or ignoring them, or transcending them. It's just the opposite. In meditation, we freely experience and realize our emotions fully – without increasing them with thought, without trying to end them or continue them, without trying to do anything about them at all.

In meditation, we don't analyze our feelings or thoughts. We let them come up, observe them fully without commenting, and let them fade away. That's all.

Usually, when we have a feeling, particularly a negative feeling, we're tempted to vent it in some way to get it off our chests. We believe that expressing it will enable us to be done with it, so that it can dissipate.

Maybe. But maybe not. In fact, it's not the expression of the feeling – that is, talking about or demonstrating the feeling – that allows it to dissipate. It's in realizing it directly – that is, in feeling it fully without adding thought to it or interfering with it – that we can truly let it go.

It's possible that unloading our feelings may help us to feel them by making them more real or intense. But this is not helpful if we then can't let them go and return to *here* and *now*.

We need to be careful. For in talking about our feelings to others, rather than just noting them completely and quietly and then letting them go, we can sometimes get caught up in them, not to mention stir up emotions in others as well. Instead of simply watching them as they dissolve, we grab hold of them and pump them up, or obsess over them. Often, as part of this process, we imagine events from our past or fantasize about our future. These reveries are never real, but we tend not to notice that. Whether they're based on memory, hope, fear, or dread, we're imagining them. They're delusional. They're not *here* and *now*.

Yet look at the power such thoughts have to carry us away.

Imagine that you drop in on a friend who's been feeling down lately, to see how he's doing. He tells you, 'I feel great today. Yesterday I wasn't doing too well, but today I'm just fine.'

'You weren't feeling well yesterday?' you ask. 'Tell me more about that.'

He does, and soon he's back in his depression.

This is exactly what we do with ourselves when we allow our thoughts to work on our emotions. Even though we might feel fine in this moment, our minds drift into the past or future, where our thoughts stir up negative feelings, say, in response to our mental images. Then, instead of letting those feelings and images drift away, we take hold of them, turn them over, and review them closely, telling ourselves more about how bad we feel.

We tend to think that by analyzing our feelings – particularly our painful ones – or the images we conjure up in our minds that engender them, we can find some core to our mental problems, get a good look at what's wrong, and then fix everything. We imagine there's something warped or bent out of shape in our minds that needs to be repaired, and, if left unattended, the disturbing or painful feelings will continue indefinitely.

But simply feeling bad is not the problem. It's this process of needing to fix what isn't broken that's the problem.

Simply feeling bad at times is normal. So is simply feeling good.

When we feel good for no particular reason, however, we rarely say to ourselves, 'Why am I feeling good? I need to figure this out, look deep within, and try to find a reason for these good feelings.' We're more likely to just let ourselves feel good and not give it another thought.

We can (and ought to) do the same with emotions we don't like: experience them completely – that is, notice them, but without trying to control or resist them. Just let them wash through and fade away.

Our problem is not that we're warped or broken at the core. Our problem is that we get caught up in our thinking. Instead of simply feeling, we mentally obsess *about* those feelings, and then confuse these thoughts with Reality. We grasp the fleeting feeling and hang on, continuing to relive our painful thoughts over and over. While we're mentally fixated on an event that took place yesterday, or last week, or twenty years ago, the actual, fresh, clean, vibrant reality of *this moment* flashes by without our even noticing.

In *this moment*, there's no dragging out our past. There's no projecting the future, with all its attendant worries, excitement, dread, regrets, and expectations.

137

This isn't to say that we ought to ignore the past or the future. But we need to understand that the past and future are never *here* but only as thought. It's always *now*; it's never then or when. *Now* is where everything takes place.

We all have a great deal of learning and experience in our memories and thoughts. Use them, but use them wisely. As my teacher used to say, 'Put them in your backpack and carry them lightly.' Let your past inform your life, not hold sway over it. Draw upon your past only as you need to, as experience and learning that can be helpful in *this moment*.

Sometimes we imagine our past as a massive weight on our shoulders, under which we must somehow lumber down the road of life. But the past simply isn't *here*. It can't be. Our *thoughts* about the past may appear in this moment, but thoughts don't have any intrinsic weight of their own. To whatever degree we imagine the weight of the past on our shoulders, it's weight that we're needlessly loading on ourselves. There's no such weight. It's only that we *think* there is.

The same goes for the future. If you dread it, you're forgetting that it's only thought. On the other hand, if you're filled with great expectations, you've just set yourself up for a big letdown. In the meantime, how much of your precious time are you going to let slip by without noticing?

Sometimes, too, the more we talk about our feelings, the more solid and permanent they appear. We fuel those feelings with thought, giving birth to them anew in each new moment. In this way we make ourselves quite miserable. We then grow attached to these feelings, believing that the stronger we feel them, the more powerful or important or profound they are. We overlook that it was in our carelessness that we artificially made them so intense. But if we carry on in this way, is it because we're capable of feeling deeply, or because we're, to some degree, insane? We're not noticing our part in all of this confusion.

We may imagine that if we talk about how we feel and why, we can get down to something genuine and true. But we can't. We can't ever really explain how we feel – we can only *feel* how we feel. This is as far as we can go without our thoughts otherwise making a mess of it.

Had we simply let our initial feeling alone, it would soon fade away like the morning dew. And our sense of urgency – our need to somehow deal with the feeling – would evaporate as well.

So in meditation we put our effort into coming back. In each moment, learn to spot yourself forming and running off into the past or the future. Then come back. Just come back. Don't say anything, not even to yourself.

We commonly imagine that thoughts and feelings are separate things. But they're not exactly, as we've seen. They constantly feed each other.

Sometimes you'll hear someone describe themselves as a thinking person or a feeling person, but the fact is, we all think and we all feel. None of us just thinks or just feels. This is directly experienced by all of us. Thinking and feeling occur together at once. Heart and mind are not separate. (Indeed, there's a classic Zen text that identifies them as one in its title: 'Trusting the Heartmind.')

In meditation, we give full attention to direct experience – that is, what we feel, see, think, hear, smell, or taste right *now*. That's all. In other words, we don't comment on it. We don't ignore it or squelch it or analyze it or dwell on it or control it. Thus it all washes through.

In learning to come into *this moment*, we realize feelings directly, and we see the thoughts that often come attached to them. But we don't judge them or talk about them. We don't make anything of them at all. They come and go, and we taste them fully and directly, with no aftertaste. We don't consume them, and they don't consume us.

We only need to watch. Negative emotions under wordless observation cannot last for long. As long as we don't say anything to ourselves about them, they will naturally weaken and die away. But if we feed and amplify those feelings, they will just as naturally remain and grow.

Our emotions and thoughts are like the weather. They are sometimes pleasant, sometimes unpleasant, always changing. We can do little to control them directly, and are wise not to try. Yet they needn't control us, either. What we can do is be alert. Just observe and let them be what they are. And after the occasional, inevitable storm has passed, we only need to quietly watch as the clouds dissipate on their own without any help from us.

25. Compassion and Candor

When calamity strikes – a tsunami wipes out thousands of miles of populated coastline, planes filled with people and fuel strike the World Trade Center, a hurricane ravages a city of over a million people – we all react strongly. Our hearts go out to all the people whose loved ones were lost or injured. We feel for and with these people, and we want to do something to help.

It's only natural that we would react in this way, and we're right to offer our help. But it's a kind of emotional roller-coaster ride. Something happens and we react.

Yet in between such events, we often look away. After a few weeks go by – when we have given our donations and the story no longer appears on the evening news – our attention to the crisis fades. Once again we become completely caught up with our own immediate concerns, our own little lives, tuning out much of the rest of the world.

Compassion isn't something that wells up in us now and then, triggered by some particular event. True compassion is steady and strong, like the flow of a river. It's not a temporary emotional scramble in response to a specific situation. It doesn't fade when a crisis has passed.

In meditation, we come to *see* that *every* moment is life

and death – that we actually live with these two merged all the time.

The situation we're in is always critical, and in each moment there's something urgent for us to do: wake up.

Compassion and wisdom arise together. In fact, they're inseparable, just as life and death are inseparable. For there to be true compassion, we need to *see* what our situation truly is. This *seeing* is wisdom, and compassion is the natural action and speech that come from that *seeing*. Thus, when we're genuinely in *this moment*, wisdom and compassion are naturally present.

In practice, this means we don't get caught in questions like 'why me?' and 'what did I do to deserve this?' or even 'why them?' Self-pity and feeling sorry for others are not compassion. They're a form of judgment, of setting yourself apart. Indeed, such questions don't even occur to us – or, if they do, we understand immediately that trying to answer them only yields more confusion. We *see* that the story is not just – or even primarily – about us.

True compassion doesn't come from a desire to help others, but from something much larger. True compassion is more a matter of how you take care of your life from day to day. How you remove your coat as you come in. How you shut the door. Everything we do can be done with the heart of compassion, but only if we're truly present. And again, this is meditation.

People often have certain expectations about their meditation teacher. We may tell ourselves that we expect the teacher to be compassionate and wise. These are, in fact, two primary qualifications of a good meditation teacher – but often what we actually expect is that the teacher will be nice to us and won't mess with our agenda.

But compassion isn't niceness (though at times the two certainly can appear together). And if niceness is what you're really after, then don't bother looking for a good meditation teacher. Just find someone who will tell you what you want to hear. Meditation is about frankness and honesty. We don't have to be brutal, but we do have to be honest.

Chögyam Trungpa said that the function of a teacher is to insult you. That may be a little too blunt, but if you're working with a capable teacher who really wants to help you wake up, they won't necessarily talk to you in a sweet and gentle voice all the time. A genuine teacher isn't concerned with your personal agenda. They don't really care whether or not you like them, or even whether or not they like you. Their concern is that you wake up. And they may be very candid and direct – that is, not nice – in helping you to do so. So be grateful if you're lucky enough to find someone like this.

Sooner or later, we all need to look unflinchingly at ourselves. Invariably this means we're going to be shown some things we don't want to see. It's best if you uncover these for yourself, but most of us need a little help. That's part of a meditation teacher's job, so don't take it personally.

A compassionate teacher will, one way or another,

bring your clinkers to your attention and invite you to sit down and really take a good look at them. Waking up means, more than anything else, that we learn to *see* ourselves.

26. What We Come to Realize

Just take up this practice of meditation. Forget reasons for and against it. Forget goals and outcomes. Forget potential gain and loss. Forget everything you think about meditation. Just return to *here* and *now*.

Meditation is stepping into *this moment* for no reason, no purpose, no ulterior motive.

In practicing meditation, you will come to understand something that is truly profound and liberating – something that you'll not find any other way.

Meditation is not about putting your finger on some holy truth. It's not that at all. It's about your attitude toward life.

When you genuinely practice meditation, you're not practicing for yourself. Though it may look like you're simply sitting (or walking) quietly, meditation is anything but a selfish act. It's an act of generosity and virtue. When we are non-grasping, non-judgmental, and not occupied with self or gain, this is a gift to others and to the world. And this activity makes the world a little more peaceful.

One day you will realize that you've known this all along.

This gift is not a particular thing you're handing anyone. Nor do you necessarily know who is receiving this gift. In fact, all such considerations are none of your business. Your business is simply to come back to *this moment*.

Eventually, you will practice meditation without a lot of ideas about it – even the idea that you're benefiting anyone through it. You'll just drop it all and come back, over and over, to *here* and *now*.

Yet the human mind is such that we can turn even this into something to go after. We might think, 'I've been sitting now for quite a while without any thought of gain! Cool! I'm getting closer!' Yet we know what to do when we catch ourselves doing this. We just let go and come back. Eventually we learn to drop such mind games altogether.

Ultimately, when we catch ourselves doing *anything* except returning to *now* and *here*, we just come back. Let go and come back.

Almost everyone takes up meditation with a leaning mind and an unwholesome attitude. Most of us first begin to truly understand meditation long after we first begin practicing it – usually after a decade or more. It certainly took me many years – and I'm still learning.

We usually come to meditation for the wrong reasons, out of ignorance and greed. This is normal. Yet, if we learn to take it up properly, if we stay with it, we see for ourselves what meditation really is. We come to see that life is not found in reaching for the next moment, but in living fully in *this moment*.

We also come to see that there's no end to meditation. There's no finish line, no graduation ceremony, no point when we're fully ripe and ready to pick, or baked to perfection and ready to remove from the oven.

There's never a time when you're done with meditation and you stop. There's no end to this practice, or to its refinement.

How could there be? There's no end (or beginning) to *here* and *now*.

PART THREE

For the Long Run

Rest your frontal lobe.

– Dainin Katagiri

27. Meditation Without Doing

One day, zen teacher Sekito Kisen came upon his student, Yakusan Igen, as he sat in meditation. Sekito asked, 'What are you doing?'

Yakusan replied, 'I'm not doing anything.'

'Then you are just sitting idly,' said Sekito.

'If I were sitting idly,' said Yakusan, 'then I'd be doing something.'

'You say you're not doing anything. What is it that you're not doing?' asked Sekito.

'Even buddhas don't know,' said Yakusan.

How often can we honestly say, 'I'm not doing anything'? And what would be that state of mind if we were truly not doing anything?

Yakusan is speaking of a state of mind that even the awakened do not know, because they're not possessed of ideas. The awakened hold no ideas of enlightenment, while those of us who are deluded often have a lot of ideas about enlightenment.

There's great subtlety in being fully present, but few of us truly realize this because, even though we might think, say, and feel we're not doing anything, actually, we're still doing. By our inattention, we insert things into our 'not-doing.' We hold ideas and beliefs. Thus we don't *just sit* in meditation. We think. In short, we maintain views.

So what is true not-doing? What is this quiet mind even buddhas don't know? Of course, I can't really tell you – that would be doing something again – but, having asked the question, you can look at it for yourself. In doing so, you may begin to notice something important about the nature of delusion.

We put together a world in our mind. We carry all kinds of ideas, beliefs, notions, and prejudices – and, for most of us, that is our reality. It's where we live. Yet it rarely occurs to most of us that we're making it all up, that we've got a major role in creating that seemingly objective world 'out there.'

When we sit down in meditation, it doesn't take very long before we can notice just how much stuff our mind is spinning and churning out. What the awakened *see* is how that moment-by-moment manufacturing takes place in our minds, and how we are easily taken in and confused by it.

We regularly confuse what we believe with what we actually *know*. Yet what we truly *know* isn't anything we could possibly think, because what we truly *know* is necessarily nonconceptual. For example, while there's direct experience of touch, taste, sight, and sound, our concept of sweet is not sweet. Our idea of hot is not hot.

This may seem mysterious, but it's not. It's as simple as eating a peach. Therein is actual Knowledge. It's not in descriptions, models, ideas, or explanations, but in direct experience – in tasting, smelling, eating. There and only there, in the immediacy of taste and texture, do we find true Knowledge.

Of course, quite apart from actual Knowledge, we can have an *idea* of eating a peach. We can recall (or imagine) flavor, fragrance, and texture. But this is not eating a peach, as your nose, tongue, and stomach will readily confirm. Yet we so often fix on the idea of eating a peach, even while we're eating a peach.

Reality simply never goes into words or ideas. At best, words can only point. They can never be what they name. Though we may ask, 'What does a peach taste like?' we can never *know* by way of an explanation. Only direct experience will remove that question from our minds. And, of course, our concern for what it's *like* vanishes as well. We don't need to ask what it's *like*. We already *know* directly.

True Knowledge is simply *thus*. The rest is packaging.

From the start, we already *know* Truth. This would be clear and obvious if only we didn't package experience in concepts and get caught in thought. There's no mystery involved, either. If we allow direct experience to flow through without trying to take hold of it, what's to be grasped? And if nothing needs to be grasped, where's the mystery?

Reality thus never validates – and never *can* validate – any conceptual view of any kind. Whether we're Christian, Jew, Muslim, or Buddhist, we can't hold up our view and legitimately claim, 'This is how it is.' 'This is Truth.' 'This is Real.' Just as any idea of eating a peach falls short of Reality, so will any idea of God, the soul, the self, paradise, life after death, Nirvana, or enlightenment.

It's very important that we understand this and stop arguing with others about what's wrong with their views, and instead reflect upon how tightly we hold on to our own. We can all see how the other person's views are invalid. What's more urgent and more difficult is that we *see* how our own cherished views are no different, that they are just as limited and flighty.

We readily confuse our beliefs with Reality. This is our most basic doing. When formed out of our egoistic desires, our beliefs not only sow immense sorrow in our personal lives, they have far-reaching consequences, to which the horrendous events of September 11, 2001, attest.

While what buddhas don't know can be found only in thought, True Knowledge is not found among ideas of doing or non-doing — yet it's fully accessible to us all in every moment if we would only be still enough to notice.

28. Where We Lose Our Way

The great eighth-century zen teacher Pai-chang said:

> Don't seek virtue, knowledge, intellectual understanding,
> and so forth. When feelings of defilement and purity are
> ended, still don't hold to this non-seeking and consider it
> right – do not dwell at the point of ending, and do not
> long for heavens or fear hells. When you are unhindered
> by bondage or freedom, this is called liberation of mind
> and body in all places.

On another occasion, Pai-chang said:

> A buddha [an awakened person] is one who does not
> seek; seek *this* and you turn away. The principle is the
> principle of non-seeking; seek it and you lose it. If you
> cling to non-seeking, this is the same as seeking; if you
> cling to non-doing, this is the same as doing.

It's the act of seeking that's the problem, not the object
being sought. This is where, sooner or later, all of us get
stuck.

Both consciously and unconsciously, all of us seek for
a very long time. This is normal and natural, since everything in our culture is built around the premise of going

after something else. It's so deeply ingrained in us that for many years (and usually for decades), we can't help ourselves.

Most of us begin practicing meditation with a seeking mind. We want to become enlightened, or at least to obtain a calmer state of mind. After a few years, we may loosen our grip on these – but we keep on seeking. In time we learn to aim at more subtle things like nonattachment.

Eventually we realize the folly and futility of seeking *anything* in meditation. But then we may start seeking non-seeking and clinging to non-clinging. We haven't fundamentally changed. We're still doing the same thing we've habitually done for decades. We've just hooked different objects on to our seeking.

We need to stop seeking and clinging. Not just to things on the 'disapproved' list. We need to stop seeking and clinging, period. This is awakening.

There is another place where every meditator gets hung up, sooner or later. This place doesn't even exist, yet it's one of the most common snares. It's a place we make up, a place we imagine exists. It goes by many different names – typically 'enlightenment,' 'wisdom,' 'awakening,' and so on. But they're all versions of 'there' – that imaginary place separate from *this moment*. We may even create an imaginary place that we label 'the present moment' – and then try to get to it by doing something other than return-ing to *here* and *now*.

There appears an infinitude of theres, but there's only one *here*. If we seek something 'out there' that will carry us to enlightenment, we're making the same old mistake.

It's all the same error, the same habit. We turn away from *here* and look to 'there.' Yet even to seek to return to *here* and *now* separates us from here and now.

If we've wondered why we find awakening so elusive, Pai-chang has just given us a big clue. It's because we're looking for it. And if we're looking for it, that means we believe it's not *here*. Consciously or unconsciously, we imagine that it's 'out there' somewhere – in a place that literally doesn't exist. Is it any wonder that it eludes us?

All the teachings of the awakened are not about what's 'out there.' There is no 'out there.' The teachings of the awakened all direct us back to *here*.

You are already *here*. Why seek to be where you are?

'So, okay,' you say, 'I'm hung up. I'm stuck. I admit it. Now what? How do I get unstuck?'

This is a third place where all of us eventually get stuck: trying to get unstuck. Some of us get stuck here for a long time. Indeed, trying to get unstuck eventually becomes our central delusion. In seeking freedom, we lose it.

So stop trying. Just be stuck.

There's only one way to practice non-seeking: by not seeking. This may sound obvious and tautological and perhaps even silly, but it's the truth. How do we breathe? By breathing. How do we love? By loving. How do we forgive? By forgiving.

In meditation, we ultimately learn not to be caught by either bondage or freedom. We simply *see* where we are.

*

All we really need to do is just stop. We get caught, and then, without trying, we free ourselves. We get caught again, and free ourselves again, over and over.

We need to awaken, again and again, in each new moment. And in each moment, we have a new opportunity to wake up.

It's all very simple. Either you're present or you're not. If you're genuinely present, there's nothing to seek. If you're not, then you've lost your way – in which case, simply come back.

Don't think there's anything more to meditation than this.

29. The Color of Meditation

Like everyone else who has taken it up, I used to think of meditation as something distinct. It had a name, a form, a look, a time, a place, and a purpose. Then there was all that other stuff – working, eating, sleeping, playing, daydreaming – loosely thought of as 'not meditation.' It seemed to me that I was either meditating or I was doing something else. It was as if I came with an internal meditation switch I was supposed to snap on whenever I entered the meditation hall, but left switched off the rest of the time.

I saw my life as a continuum. At one end, I assumed my birth. At the other end, I imagined my death. Each event in my life could be represented as a dot on that continuum with its location marking a specific time.

As part of this common but erroneous view, I saw meditation as just one more thing – one more set of recurring events – that appeared as, say, blue dots every once in a while amid other colored dots (representing other kinds of events) along the continuum of my life.

The tiny blue dots were separated by relatively large gaps where my meditation practice was interrupted by periods of no meditation (that is, by other activities). Like most people, I saw meditation as some special activity I *applied* to my life, rather than as life itself lived as the present moment.

When we think of meditation practice in this way, we can easily develop ideas like, 'I *should* meditate.' 'I *need* to sit.' 'I've had a rough week; maybe if I meditated more I would feel better.' 'I've had a rough week; I'm too tired to meditate now.' We can go anywhere with this kind of thinking, but it's all delusion.

Here's another way to look at meditation and our lives. It's still a model – that is, it's still a conceptual repackaging of Reality – but it may be enough to give you a clearer sense of what meditation actually is.

First of all, there's no continuum of life running from past to present to future. Life is all at once. Not stretched over time, but *now*. (This is, after all, what we actually experience. At one o'clock, it's *now*. At nine o'clock, it's *now*. It's forever *now*. It's never 'then.')

And there aren't any blue dots at all. Rather, as we take up meditation, it appears that the whole of our life begins to blue – pale at first, but ever deepening and darkening.

Gradually, our life takes on the color of meditation. Not as little dots (as in 'now I'm meditating; now I'm not'), but as an ever-deepening tone that permeates everything.

Meditation isn't something we take up for an hour and then drop and forget about until it shows up again on our schedule. It isn't some extracurricular activity we come back to sporadically whenever the thought or the urge or the mood strikes. It isn't something that involves dashing off to the meditation hall, taking a seat, mentally clocking in when the bell rings, and clocking out again when the bell rings again later.

If you understand meditation as the unfolding of your life, and allow your life to simply be the color of meditation, then there's never a time when 'this is meditation' and other times when 'this is not.'

Meditation is *now* or not at all.

When meditation is merely some technique we apply to our life, as if it were a self-improvement course, eventually we grow frustrated and weary of it. If, however, we cultivate meditation steadily from the heart, then the quality of our mind and heart, and the way we conduct our life will begin to change. Instead of our practice being intermittent or an exercise in struggle, it becomes smooth and steady. Where we used to hit rocks in the road and shatter or bounce uncontrollably, we now more easily absorb the shock of hitting obstacles in our path. Life flows more smoothly, like a stream, rather than our getting hung up or blocked as we try to remove or steer clear of obstacles.

We find it easier to establish regular times in our schedule for formal meditation, where we do nothing but sit, breathe, and return to where we are – *here* and *now*. At the same time, we also begin to understand that other activities in our life – our job, our interactions with family and friends, our time with difficult people – all become part of our meditation practice. Our life takes on the color of meditation. With this gradual deepening and diffusion, meditation spreads throughout our life.

30. Where to Put Your Energy

Meditation involves putting your energy into the entire field and fabric of life, rather than burning it out in points and particles of self-interest.

Most of us focus habitually on the particles – the specifics – that make up our world. In meditation, however, we learn to do the opposite – to *see* the field of life as well as the particles that make it up.

Kosho Uchiyama, a Japanese Zen teacher who died in 1998, wrote a wonderful book called *How to Cook Your Life: From the Zen Kitchen to Enlightenment*. In it he points out that it's fundamental that we put our energy into the whole of life, rather than let some single issue or view carry us away.

We easily get caught up in our own narrow ego issues. Most of the time, we're tuned in to our favorite radio station, WIFM – What's Init For Me – which provides us with endless talk about 'my wants,' 'my needs,' 'my goals,' 'our agenda,' and so on.

In part, we've been conditioned to be relentlessly narrow and ego-focused in this way by the fast-paced commercial culture in which we live. But we also condition ourselves to stay narrow by habitually seeing ourselves as cut off from everything that we believe is 'out there.' Thus we become preoccupied with pleasing our dear little self and focusing on our own narrow self-interest.

Uchiyama invites us to step back a little. Instead of letting some particular pet issue carry us away – 'this is my goal, my purpose, my mission in life' – he urges us to put our energy into the Wholeness of life.

If you look carefully, you'll discover that the road to true happiness doesn't take us through the land of Getting-What-I-Want. Nor does it cross the territory of Achieving-My-Goals. Instead, the road to true happiness leads us out of our own point of view, our own narrow self-interest.

It's precisely because the particular and the narrow stand out in stark relief against a flurried background of other things that we're so easily caught by them. And thus we're readily consumed by longing and loathing. Without some reflection, we'll inevitably put our energy there. It's easy for us to do this. It's not so easy for us to put our energy into what is not point-like – that is, to turn our mind away from the particular to the life of the Whole.

In meditation, however, when we slip into self-interest and lose sight of the Whole, we just bring ourselves back to Reality, to Wholeness. We learn to notice when we've entered a narrow space where 'me,' 'my,' and 'mine' become our focus. And we also begin to *see* that our true interests lie not within the narrow confines of the self, but with the Whole.

It's in watching and noticing the way the boundless world actually works, beyond all our petty concerns for personal gain, that we at last realize our true heart: clarity, contentment, healthy-mindedness, and peace.

31. At Home in the World

When you practice meditation with other people, your meditation has a profound effect on those others, encouraging and supporting them. This is true even if at first you can't feel it – and even if no one says anything about it.

This works both ways, of course: in meditating with others, their presence also supports and encourages you.

When I first began meditating with others, I felt very encouraged by their presence and practice, but it took awhile for me to realize how this effect went both ways.

This tells us something essential about the nature of meditation practice – and, indeed, about who we are as creatures living on this planet. We are all in this together, whether we acknowledge it or not.

As we learn to engage fully and directly in what we're doing, we have a profound effect on others, by encouraging them to take up their lives in the same manner. Indeed, although it may not always be evident, everything we do has a profound influence on others.

With practice, meditation will show us something else: that we can't locate where anything takes place.

Smell a flower. Where does that experience take place? In the flower? In your nose? In your mind? Do such questions even make sense?

And where does your mind take place?

Without giving it careful consideration, we may quickly blurt out that our experience is somehow in our heads. And yet, clearly, we are sensing things that *seem* to be 'out there' somehow.

So where *is* *this* happening? We can't really locate it. This gives us a big clue about the nature of mind and experience, though it goes mostly unnoticed by nearly everyone. Even after it has been pointed out, we tend to become confused by the question, or we quickly forget about it.

Gradually, as we become more experienced with meditation, we start to realize that awareness isn't just gathered around a 'me here.' Awareness includes everything. It's more an Awareness that there's no 'around' and nothing particular that is 'you.' It's all *here* in the experience of *this moment*.

Thus we eventually *see* for ourselves that we never meditate alone. In fact, there is no 'by myself.' In fully realizing this, loneliness disappears, and our meditation no longer has any taint of ego or greed.

We also begin to see how our notions of a self have until now relentlessly bullied and driven our mind with its load of ideas, fears, attitudes, and prejudices. This fixation on 'me' now begins to be seen for what it is – delusion and a source of pain.

Gradually, we also begin to resist meditation less. Maintaining a steady practice becomes more natural because we realize we're not doing it alone. Indeed, in a sense, *we're* not doing it at all – that is, there's no 'us' here and 'the practice of meditation' over there. Meditation ceases to be something we make a personal effort to do. More and more, we realize that our life is inseparable from the life of the World.

This realization alters our practice in profound ways. We no longer think in terms of what we're getting out of it or how it benefits ourselves or anyone else. We've learned to sit as the World sits: in quietness and stillness. Our simple, silent meditation now expresses the life of the Universe.

Our life really is the life of the World. Our life is not our own, and true happiness is not ours to pursue. Nevertheless, it will overtake us if we let it. In forgetting yourself, you're never alone.

With a mind cultivated in meditation, we are thus at home and at ease in the World.

32. Sounding Silence

Why do we maintain silence during meditation? Because silence is essential to awakening.

Just as the world is constant activity around a center of stillness, it is also sound around a center of silence.

Silence is not the absence of sound. Silence frames all sounds. Sound and silence are thus inseparable. We cannot have one without the other. Silence is the backdrop of everything, and everything returns to silence.

In meditation, we can *know* this directly for ourselves.

Yet many of us are unsettled, or threatened, or even terrified by silence. Often when we're with people, particularly people we've just met, we feel uncomfortable just to sit with them in silence.

And it's not only 'external' silence that disturbs us. We also commonly feel the need to keep our minds occupied, never allowing them to go silent.

When we sit down in meditation, most of us immediately discover that our minds are filled with a lot of mental noise. And the more internal noise we make, the more additional mental noise we make in response to it.

Most of us try to flee from silence whenever the moment begins to settle into it. We compulsively fill our lives with noise and activity. We turn on the radio or the

TV, hoping to occupy ourselves and to drive back the surrounding silence. And that's exactly what happens: these stimuli take over our minds, like a country being occupied by an invading army. Yet without reflection, we would prefer this mental havoc to the silence of *here* and *now*, which we imagine to be terribly disturbing.

But *here* and *now* are not inherently disturbing or frightening. It's only when we're *out of this moment* and lost in our imagination that we're so disturbed. When we're actually *in this moment*, it's anything but disturbing – and it's certainly not frightening.

In meditation, we lose our fear of silence. Rather, we become intimate with it – as with an old friend.

Mental noise can lead us down a very slippery slope, particularly if we forcefully try to quiet our mind. Often people will be disturbed by their thoughts because they think the assignment in meditation is to quiet their mind. 'My thoughts drive me crazy,' they will say. But the more you try to control your thoughts, whether with a club or a drug, the noisier and bossier they're going to become.

In meditation we get off this merry-go-round. We don't try to squelch or soothe or negotiate with our thoughts. We simply watch them and let them be what they are. If they constitute a boiling cauldron, we watch them boil without judgment or comment. Whether hateful or lovely, shocking or serious, or just plain drivel, we observe our thoughts silently – that is, without engaging them.

In this way, we express and experience silence even in the midst of our own inner turmoil. When we truly let our thoughts be, without being disturbed by their churning energy, they will simmer down on their own. We need not do anything to them or about them other than just watch them. In this way we can know them for what they are – just thoughts.

The same is true of 'external' noise.

'Quiet, please, I'm meditating' is a contradiction in terms. In meditation we allow, without judgment or control, whatever appears, whether it boils up in our thoughts or wafts in through the window. If, as you sit in meditation, a car alarm goes off, a lawn mower starts up, or a crowd of loud and boisterous people decide to have a conference outside your window, simply let it all be part of the experience. Don't try to block it out. Don't get all worked up about it. Don't even think about it. It's not necessary to leave off with meditation as if you're supposed to do something about it. What is there to do?

As we meditate, we don't demand that the world be silent around us. That would just be another variation on our old theme of 'I'm not satisfied, so I need to rearrange the world.' And, anyway, we can't make the world silent, no matter how hard we try. Sometimes noisy things happen just outside your window, no matter what you do. Meditation is just to be there with what is happening. There's no need for you to control any of it.

Of course, it makes sense to hold formal meditation in a place that is generally quiet and calm. That would be suitable, but not mandatory. Sometimes the world simply won't be calm and quiet, regardless of our efforts. We can let things be however they are and simply pay attention – particularly to our own mind. This is the task at hand.

If we know how to keep silence properly, we can maintain silence even while speaking and acting.

Just as Dogen noted that 'meditation has nothing what-ever to do with sitting or lying down,'[4] real silence has nothing whatever to do with the lack of sound. It has to do with your mind. We can meditate while we walk, or work, or play. With an alert, fully present mind, we can thus express silence while talking, or singing, or even clearing our throat.

Silence is of the mind and heart. It doesn't issue from anywhere in particular. Thus, with a mind of silence, you can talk or act without ever straying from *here* and *now*.

Whenever we are out of the moment, we have a noisy mind. But a mind that is awake, alert, and fully present with *this moment* already expresses silence.

It is in this silence that the world speaks directly to us.

In the woods, if you make a lot of noise, you'll see very little wildlife. But if you're quiet and still, the natural world reveals itself to you. The life of the world that otherwise

---

[4] The actual term Dogen used in place of 'meditation,' as I've rendered it, was *sanzen*. Sanzen, in this context, refers to meditation (zazen), properly carried out.

remains hidden from us will come forward and join us in universal silence and stillness.

Like so, in meditation, by simply letting the mind be what it is, without adding any words, the world reveals itself to us in silence.

33. Meditation Without Gimmicks

This chapter is about finding our way into the more subtle aspects of meditation – those that rarely get discussed.

It's nearly impossible to talk about them without getting bogged down in semantic and conceptual glue. Words and concepts can't really convey these aspects of meditation. So please hold lightly the words that follow, with an understanding that they abound with potential traps and snares.

As we look at – and practice – meditation, we will come to ever deeper and more subtle understanding. Our initial insights aren't necessarily forbidden, but with practice and proper attention, they will naturally give way to a subtler yet more expansive awareness. We can illustrate this process on a continuum:

more simplistic and   *more subtle and*
←conceptual understanding   *profound awareness→*

Most of the things that meditation teachers teach can also be placed on this same continuum, with cruder, more simplistic instructions and techniques on the left and more subtle and less conceptual ones on the right.

Even though the crude instructions don't really hit

the mark, people new to meditation – and many meditation teachers – like to use them because they're more
graspable. They're easily presented in the familiar ways
in which we commonly think. These are instructions
and techniques that make use of objects. It makes us feel
better – like we're getting somewhere – if we can get
hold of something, even though such teachings bind us
in our usual dualistic understanding of self and other.

As we gain experience and refine our understanding,
however, we may wake up to what cannot be grasped.
Indeed, if we don't get bogged down too far to the left on
this continuum, we can actually come to *see* what cannot
be grasped at all – that is, the far right of the continuum.

For example, consider the teaching of impermanence.
Everything changes. This seems to make sense to us once
our attention is drawn to it. As we examine the world, we
notice that we can't point to anything that is not subject to
incessant change – and, ultimately, dissolution. This
includes our bodies, our homes, our neighborhoods, even
the Earth itself. Furthermore, our thoughts, our feelings, and
even our minds are equally impermanent – ever changing,
never holding still. This is how nearly all of us first understand impermanence. This is how impermanence appears
to us when we're on the left end of the continuum where
it's easily grasped.

As we look more deeply, however, we may move toward
the right along the continuum and begin to notice far
more subtle aspects of impermanence that were not pre-
viously apparent to us. As we develop a more refined
understanding of impermanence, we begin to *see* that, in

Reality, *nothing* is impermanent. Impermanence is *so* complete, *so* thorough, that nothing is formed in the first place to *be* impermanent. Were we taught this at first, however, we would likely be baffled or upset or simply dismissive of it. We can't *find* the right end of the continuum if we approach it straight on, so we don't start people out on the right end. Rather, we come onto the continuum at some point further to the left and then move to the right as we refine our understanding.

Placed on this continuum, then, these particular understandings might look like this:

←*everything is impermanent*   *nothing is impermanent*→

The same is true with meditation instruction. This is why, in Chapter 10, we didn't start out too far to the right. It's too subtle, too hard to *see* right away. It's best to start at a point a bit further to the left where you can at least *find* an object – in this case, the breath.

This poses a problem, however: the crude end of the continuum is very sticky. In fact, the left end of the continuum, where we would make use of most objects, is *so* sticky that you'll likely get stuck there if that's where you start out. In relying on an object you'll be so far to the left that you'll inevitably find it very difficult to move to the less sticky end of the continuum.

There are all sorts of techniques, such as visualization, trance, relaxation, or labeling thoughts and feelings, and objects, such as music, bells, mantras, candles, mandalas, colored disks or lights, sounds, thoughts, or other sensations, commonly used in meditation. These all carry with them a high degree of stickiness and thus are at or near the left end of this continuum.

Not so, the breath. As mentioned earlier (in Chapter 10), by appearing subjective and objective at once, it's a unique object in this regard – it's far less sticky by nature. The technique of simply following the breath – that is, using breath as the sole object of meditation – falls further to the right along this continuum. (*Counting* the breaths falls much further to the left and, therefore, ought to be used sparingly or not at all. It's quite sticky, and you can easily become dependent on it as with other graspable techniques. In and of itself, it's a weak technique in that it's hypnotic. Since we've all been counting as far back as we can remember, it's so automatic that we can easily count to 37 or 53 before we realize what we're doing.)

But what about the instruction or technique that appears nearest the non-sticky end of the spectrum? This is generally quite hard to find, to *see*, and to understand – at least at first. It's best not to try to approach it directly. Yet there is indeed a meditation practice that is the simplest and least sticky, and beyond which we cannot go. It's called *shikantaza* and is often simplistically translated as 'just sitting.' I'll discuss this term in some detail in Chapter 35.

On the left side of this continuum, there are many things that can bog us down. But it's also a very easy place to begin. That's why a lot of teachers work in this area. The techniques used near this end provide a wide opening for people to enter into meditation. The danger is that we easily get stuck there.

It's of utmost importance that we not get stuck. A good teacher can help us at this point so that we may realize the more subtle aspects of meditation.

My own teacher offered a narrow range of teachings along this spectrum, all very near or just at the non-sticky end. Thus, I teach in the same way, both with my students and in this book.

Here's another way to look at this same continuum:

business as usual　　　　　　　*where there*
←(stuck in delusion)　　　　　*is no further→*

If you avoid excessive stickiness and take up this practice wholeheartedly and honestly, you'll naturally realize ever more subtle aspects of meditation. And eventually you will discover a place where there's nothing to hang on to – that is, where there is no idea or technique at all.

34. No Time, Place, or Size

When zen teachers talk about *shikantaza* – 'just sitting,' without focusing on any object or process – they sometimes use the term single-pointed concentration. When we first hear this term, we might think they're speaking of something small, like a speck of dust. It seems to refer to filing our concentration down to a tiny point. But single-pointed concentration is actually quite different in that it includes the Whole World.

Single-pointed concentration is like each pixel in a hologram. It has all the information of the Whole. Indeed, if you were to fully experience *this* single dust-mote moment, you would *know* the Whole.

The thing we need to realize about *just this*, the focus of our single-pointed concentration, is that it's not a 'little' point. It's not a 'big' point either. It's a *sizeless* point.

It's called a point because it's just One. But it's truly One, with a capital 'O.' It's not one as opposed to many, or one as opposed to two or three. It's One without any other. Single-pointed concentration doesn't have any size. It doesn't have any dimension. It doesn't have any duration. It doesn't have any location. It doesn't have any object. It's *just this*. It's objectless Awareness.

With objectless Awareness, there's sound, but no object of sound. There may be the sound of a plane or of birds chirping – but it's not a plane, it's not birds. It's just sound, with nothing extra forming out of sound.

When the great Zen master Yun Men was asked, 'What is single-pointed concentration?' he said, 'Food in the bowl. Water in the bucket.'

We're easily confused by such direct talk. 'That's it? Just food in a bowl and water in a bucket?' 'What's that supposed to mean?' 'This is nonsense!' 'I don't get it.' 'This is too deep for me.'

Catch yourself. Stop *thinking* about what Yun Men said and just take it in. 'Food in the bowl, water in the bucket.' Nothing more. Stop making anything out of it. Stop talking to yourself. Crawl into what is being pointed out. Put down the book for a moment and have a direct *look* at *this*.

You're walking along a lakeshore on a warm spring morning, and a duck crosses your path. You think to yourself, 'duck.'

See if, instead, you can experience without labeling. The fact is, the moment you think 'duck,' your awareness is diminished. The direct experience is lost – bound into concepts.

If instead you wordlessly experience *this moment*, you will discover that you can always reconstruct the moment later, if you need to. But while it's happening, don't talk to yourself about it. Don't throw labels on it. Stay with what's happening. Don't try to hold on to it. Just be there, fully present with what's going on.

You might start to realize true *seeing*.

This is single-pointed concentration.

In meditation, words and concepts will spontaneously appear. Let them go. Don't hold on to them or build upon them. Don't think about them or use them to calculate some expectation. Just stay *here*.

Start cultivating a wordless Awareness of *just this*.

35. Knowing Before You Think

Shikantaza is meditation in its simplest form. There are only three elements: body, mind, and breath. No gimmicks. Nothing to hold on to. Not even the breath. Breath is still present, of course, but we're not fixed on it.

Earlier in this book I talked about tranquility (*shamatha* in Sanskrit) and awareness (*vipashyanā* in Sanskrit). In *shikantaza*, these two are not separate. The mind settles, but not on a particular point. In *shikantaza*, Awareness is objectless and subjectless – there's no 'you' who does *shikantaza*. It's as if concentration has been filed down to a single point – yet, at the same time, has expanded outward and is taking in everything: sights, sounds, feelings, sensations, thoughts, movements. And this Awareness is sizeless and timeless.

In *shikantaza* we discover that there is no clear distinction between self and other. Are you breathing? Or are you being breathed? You need not answer. There is no essential difference. Awareness is general and without location. It's been this way all along, but only now is it clear and obvious.

Shikantaza is a Japanese word made up of four parts. The first two – *shi* and *kan* – are Tranquility and Awareness. *Ta* refers to hitting the exact spot – dead on target, not one atom off – which, in this case, means that these 'two,' shi and kan, are not even merged, but rather there is no distinction to be made between them. And finally, *za* means to sit.

Shikantaza is often translated as 'just sitting.' But this label is misleading since *shikan* can involve any activity. We can know directly shikan basketball, shikan driving, or shikan dishwashing. *Shikanta* – tranquility, Awareness, hitting the mark – is not just limited to sitting meditation. All of everyday life can be lived in the spirit of shikan – 'nothing but,' *just this*.

This is a radically different emphasis from practicing meditation with the idea that it's a special activity set apart from everything else that we do. When we practice meditation with such a notion – or any notion at all, really – it can easily become brittle, narrow, and unworldly. In fact, it often becomes a form of escapism – a mental vacation.

Shikantaza is often described as 'sitting like a mountain.' Stability in your posture is absolutely critical. You just sit, quiet and still. Whatever occurs – thoughts, sounds, feelings, and sensations that come and go – are just clouds drifting by. And just as a mountain is not moved or disturbed by clouds, you don't grab hold of anything. You don't identify with anything. You don't label anything. You don't say anything about what appears or disappears. You're simply fully present.

In this tranquility of objectless, subjectless Awareness, everything drops away, yet all is affirmed.

36. Now or Never

You can only meditate *now*. Don't wait for a more auspicious time. There is no other time but *now*. When has it ever not been *now*?

Meditation is not bound in thought, and it's only when we're caught up in thought that we have notions of other times and places. But these other times and places don't truly exist. They're mental phantoms, products of our thought and speculation.

Since meditation can only be carried out *here* and *now*, you don't need to run off somewhere else – like India, Japan, Tibet, or Bulgaria – to take it up. You don't need to go to some quiet, secluded place. You don't need to go anywhere. In fact, in meditation we finally *stop* trying to go somewhere else other than *here*.

You don't have to become someone else to meditate. You don't need to wear a robe or other special clothes. You already have everything you need to take up this practice: body, mind, and breath.

'Meditation *now* or *never*' isn't a threat or a challenge or a command. It's simply how things are. When we meditate, it is always *now*. It's never 'then' or 'when.'

Of course, it's always *here* and *now* whether we meditate or not. But in meditation we live this out, rather than ignore it, fight it, deny it, or try fruitlessly to go elsewhere.

In this book I've laid out what you need to get started in meditation, and what you may encounter down the road. But, as Kosho Uchiyama points out, meditation itself is your actual teacher. You can only come to a full understanding of this by living it.

This book has shown you a doorway. I'm pointing to it *now*. But you're the one who has to walk through.

Epilogue

It's Up to You

Meditation isn't something we *apply* to our life. Rather, we take it up *as* our life. We cultivate it with our whole heart. It usually takes time to settle into a meditation practice, so be patient with yourself.

Almost anything else you can do is much more fun and exciting than maintaining a steady meditation practice. This is why the desire to practice seriously and daily generally doesn't sink into us until we've been meditating for several years. But once it does sink in, it sinks in deeply.

If you can, find a good meditation teacher. But a poor teacher may be worse than no teacher at all. And while the guidance of a good meditation teacher is helpful, we can't rely on someone else to awaken us, or to give us a magic wisdom pill.

It's not the teacher's responsibility to motivate you to meditate. Meditation is maturity of mind. No one else can wake up for you. It all depends on your own aspiration. This is how it is for everyone – you, me, your meditation teacher, the Buddha, and everyone else on Earth, past, present, and future.

As Kosho Uchiyama has pointed out, you must have

within yourself your own aspiration to practice meditation. Whether you wake up or sleep through life depends upon your own aspiration.

Finally, don't take everything you hear about meditation – even this book – on faith. Test things out. Trust your own experience. *You* are the final authority. You must *see* and *know* for yourself what is genuine and true.

What each of us needs most is to be awake. That's all. It's enough.

What to Look for in a Meditation Teacher

First of all, a teacher must practice, daily and visibly, and have been doing so for at least ten years. Twenty years is much better. Thirty years, better still.

A true teacher won't try to sell you anything or convince you of anything – least of all the goodness or rightness of meditation. They won't use a lot of gimmicks and gadgetry to entice you, either. Nor will they have any interest in controlling or manipulating you in any way. In fact, they may even seem indifferent to you, because a good meditation teacher knows that you have to come to this practice on your own.

A true teacher doesn't want you to worship them or to come to them for guidance, as if their job is to steer your life. A meditation teacher is not a counselor. They can clarify a few things regarding this practice, point out the shoals, and give you tips on navigating through rough water, but the rest is up to you.

A good teacher will not put you in a position where you need to rely on them. And don't expect the teacher to bestow something upon you. In fact, as my own teacher,

Dainin Katagiri, told me, 'The final job of the teacher is to free the student of the teacher.'

Similarly, a good teacher won't need *you*. They won't need (or expect) you to stay with them, and they won't be personally invested in what you do or the choices you make. A true teacher won't try to make you into something you're not, especially not a trophy or a plaything of their own.

If you find a good teacher, you have to give up on expecting anything from them. The best ones won't give you anything. They'll just demonstrate the life of meditation day after day. It's up to you to pay attention. So stop thinking about yourself and just practice meditation following your teacher's example.

If you do find a good teacher, don't go to them with a lot of ideas about what you expect them to do for you. If you're preoccupied with your own agenda, you won't hear or see what the teacher is pointing out.

It's not uncommon for a student to work with a teacher for some months or years, all the while clinging to their own agenda or expectations. Then, when things don't unfold in the way the student expected, they get angry and blame the teacher. But the problem isn't the teacher; it's the student's naïve, unfounded, or ill-formed hopes and projections.

Many of us also get stuck on our ideas about what a meditation teacher should be like. They think that a meditation teacher should only drink tea and eat brown rice, or that they can get by on very little sleep, or that they can walk on water.

A good teacher ought to be morally upright, certainly. But, by the same token, so should you.

Even so, don't be alarmed by an occasional stumble. One misstep needn't sever your relationship. Anyway, it's not that a teacher, or any human being, should never stumble, but that they should immediately get back on their feet. Just as meditation is about coming back to *here* and *now*, the measure of our practice is in how quickly we get back on the right path when we stray from it.

Of course, if the teacher's infraction is great, or if they persist in it, or if they operate a program of deceit or take advantage of students, then perhaps you should leave them. But I would neither go looking for flaws nor put blinders on. If you do learn of serious misconduct by the teacher, however, you owe it to them to confront them.

You need to trust your meditation teacher. Don't work with anyone you don't trust – but don't view them with suspicion unless they give you cause, either.

Lastly, don't get the idea that things are any different for a teacher than they are for you. The most important thing about a teacher is that they are human. This means that, just like you, they have human foibles, emotions, and flaws. Without making excuses, let your teacher be human. And give yourself this same permission.

Acknowledgments

If, as the saying goes, the beginning is the half of all, I owe a great deal of thanks to Lee Register for getting this project off the ground. When I asked Lee to assist me in preparing material for this book based on my classes on meditation, he quickly supplied me with a rough draft of what became the first part of this book, as well as with the foundation for a couple of the chapters in Part Two. With Lee's kick-start I was on my way.

I want to thank Sharon Plett who transcribed from my talks more than half of the pieces that went into this book (most of Parts Two and Three). Thanks also to Hank Brooks for supplying a transcript for one of the chapters.

Thanks as well to Tom Staufenberg for producing the photos in this volume, and to Dawn Knight, Paul Lundin, and Lynn Salmon-Easter for their assistance in this project. And thanks to Jose Palmieri for his skillful editing and arranging of the photos and for much other technical assistance.

I owe a deep debt of gratitude to Kay Hanson and Bev Forsman for taking on much of the work of running Dharma Field Meditation and Learning Center that would otherwise fall to me. Without their tireless help I would not find the time to write.

Thanks also to my wife, Jean, my Dharma brother,

Norm Randolph, and Bev Forsman for their careful readings of the manuscript. They made many excellent comments and suggestions, which helped to bring this book to a finer polish.

And last, as always, I want to thank Scott Edelstein, my literary agent, editor, and longtime friend for the great deal of work he put into this book. Much of the credit I receive as a writer should go to Scott.

Selected Bibliography

Chadwick, David, ed. *To Shine One Corner of the World: Moments with Shunryu Suzuki*. New York: Broadway Books, 2001.

Cleary, Thomas, trans. and ed. *Sayings and Doings of Pai-chang: Ch'an Master of Great Wisdom*. Los Angeles: Center Publications, 1978.

Cleary, Thomas, trans. and ed. *Zen Essence: The Science of Freedom*. Boston: Shambhala, 1989.

Dogen and Kosho Uchiyama. *How to Cook Your Life: From the Zen Kitchen to Enlightenment*. Translated by Thomas Wright. Boston: Shambhala, 2005.

Dogen, 'Fukanzazengi,' trans. Norman Waddell and Abe Masao, *Eastern Buddhist* VI, no. 2 (1973): 122.

Lanza del Vasto, Joseph Jean. *Return to the Source*. New York: Simon and Schuster, 1971.